Hamlyn all-colour paperbacks

Henry Hodges
Pottery

illustrated by Eric Tenney

D0774387

Hamlyn - London
Sun Books - Melbourne

£1.50

FOREWORD

The study of porcelain has already been covered in this series of books by Eileen Aldridge, so that only the other two main sub-groups of ceramics, earthenwares and stonewares, need to be discussed in this volume. Even so, it has been necessary to restrict the field still further by omitting any but passing mention to pottery figures, busts, tiles, architectural ceramics or other purely decorative wares, save in those cases where a study of solely ornamental pottery is essential to an understanding of later developments.

A second absorbing area of study that has to be given very cursory treatment is that of social influences such as changing methods of cooking and of serving meals, modifications in table manners, fashions for metal and other non-ceramic wares, and even restrictions imposed by religious dogma. All have played their part in deciding the final shapes and decorative motifs produced by potters.

In view of the ever-increasing interest shown by the public in hand-potting and other crafts, it was felt that many readers would be just as concerned to know how and of what a vessel was made as to discover what influences dictated its shape and style of decoration. Nevertheless, it must be emphasized that this book can only serve as an introduction. A deeper understanding can only be gained by further reading, and, of even greater importance, by handling the wares themselves. If it does no more than stimulate the reader to this end, then the purpose of this book has been fully achieved.

H.W.M.H.

Published by the Hamlyn Publishing Group Limited
London · New York · Sydney · Toronto
Hamlyn House, Feltham, Middlesex, England
In association with Sun Books Pty Ltd., Melbourne

Copyright © The Hamlyn Publishing Group Limited 1972

ISBN 0 600 00293 4
Phototypeset by Filmtype Services Limited, Scarborough
Colour separations by Schwitter Limited, Zurich
Printed in Holland by Smeets, Weert

CONTENTS

WHAT IS POTTERY?

All pottery is made, partly at least, of clay which has been heated to a temperature at which it can no longer be softened by the addition of water. The clays may vary from pure white ones, such as kaolin, to blue or yellow ones, which fire red or buff. Few potters, however, use clay alone to make their wares, and other minerals are normally added as *tempers* or *fillers*. The blend of clay and temper is referred to as the *body*.

Shaping can be done in one of three ways. The first is by *modelling*. In another method the body is shaped in a *mould* which must be so designed that the vessel can be removed from it. The third way is to use some kind of *wheel* on which the clay can be made to rotate, and while it is so doing to draw it up, or *throw* it, to the required shape. Combinations of these methods may be used to make a single vessel.

In decorating wares there are many possibilities. The surface may be covered with a suspension of fine clay or *slip*; or areas may be painted with coloured slips which may themselves be made from natural clays, or coloured by the addition of pigments. More complex are the *glazes*, which are essentially glasses formed by the fusion of *silica* and a *flux*. When properly formed, glazes should make an impervious layer over the surface of the pot, but if incorrectly formulated may show a network of cracks, known as *crazing* or *crackle*, or they may peel away from the body. Other minerals may be used deliberately to colour glazes, chiefly the ores of copper (green), manganese (purple), cobalt (blue) and antimony (yellow), while the presence of tin oxide will make glazes white and opaque.

The temperature to which pottery is fired depends upon the nature of the body and the purpose to which it will be put. If it is fired below about 1200°C it remains porous and is known as *earthenware*. Some pottery, however, contains few *fluxes* and may be fired up to 1300°C, when it becomes impermeable *stoneware*. Many wares undergo more than a single firing. The first firing of the unglazed wares is referred to as the *biscuit* firing, and the second, in which the glaze is formed, the *glost*. *Enamels* are coloured glazes applied after the glost.

A potter at his wheel in the late sixteenth century.

4

Part of an Egyptian tomb painting. Beni Hasan, *c.* 1900 BC.

BEFORE THE GREEKS
The workshop emerges

The earliest pottery known was made in Anatolia well before 6000 BC where it has been found in the ruins of prehistoric villages. By 4000 BC the technique of making pottery had spread to most of the countries of the Middle East, to the Balkans and Central Europe. Initially shapes were simple, often imitating baskets, gourds and wooden containers. The surface was usually of an uneven colour due to the fact that it was fired in contact with wood fuel at a low temperature in an open hearth. Shaping was carried out either by moulding a slab of clay over an existing pot, or by building up the walls of the vessel by adding rings of clay one above the other. From the outset pottery was never made of clay alone, but of a mixture of clay with sand or crushed rock which allowed drying and firing without cracking. Usually the surface was given a smooth burnish by rubbing the dry (green-hard) shape with a pebble. Sometimes the surface was decorated by impressing a small object into it while still wet, or patterns were painted in pale clay or red or yellow ochre. Pot-making was a domestic activity demanding no specialized equipment.

By 3000 BC great social and technological changes had taken place. The increased size of the communities of the Middle East demanded ever increasing specialization, a trend from which the potter was not excluded. The evolution of a simple pivoted wheel allowed the production of more regular shapes than before, while the development of a crude up-draught kiln not only allowed the wares to be separated from the fuel but also resulted in a more even and higher firing. Egyptian tomb paintings made about 2000 BC depict quite clearly the organization of a potter's workshop at this stage of development. Here workmen can be seen 'wedging' clay by treading it; others, squatting, are 'throwing' pots on a hand-rotated wheel. The vertical kiln is loaded through the top, to which a temporary capping will later be added, while the fire is stoked through an opening at ground-level. Other workmen are fetching and carrying, while a selection of typical wares – cups, jugs and bowls – show the products of the workshop.

A potter at his wheel today. Hadramaut, Aden.

Painted pottery of the prehistoric Middle East

The majority of prehistoric pottery of the Middle East was undecorated, utilitarian earthenware. Nevertheless a great quantity of decorated pottery was manufactured of which 'painted' pottery was far the most common. Communities were scattered so that an enormous diversity of shapes and motifs evolved, varying from simple bowls and jars to elaborate vases; from decoration in geometric patterns to designs incorporating flower and animal motifs. The materials used and the methods of production, however, were remarkably uniform throughout the whole of the Middle East. Initially decoration was carried out in a clay, which was brushed on before firing, the colour of which contrasted with that of the body. Gradually other painting techniques were evolved. Clays were coloured with crushed ochre, or vessels might be covered completely with a slip of another colour before the design was painted on. Colour contrast was, however, not always achieved by painting. In Egypt, for example, red earthenwares were sometimes half-buried in ash, or painted with oil as they cooled, in order to blacken the covered areas.

Egyptian faïence

Apart from the common red and buff-firing clays of the Middle East, one other material was developed in Mesopotamia and Egypt that was ultimately (see page 47) to be of great importance. This material is generally referred to as Egyptian faïence, a misleading name since it bears no relationship whatever to faïence (see page 90) but approximates more closely to European soft-paste porcelains. In about 4000 BC, it bore no relationship to pottery at all, for it was composed of a fine quartz and cemented by a matrix of glass. A glaze of the same composition as the glass, but coloured turquoise blue with copper, was used to cover the body. In the first instance the material was probably intended to do no more than imitate the rare mineral *lapis lazuli*. Indeed, in its unfired state it was too gritty to throw satisfactorily on a wheel and it was thus normally shaped by moulding into beads and small figures. Nevertheless, cups, jars, vases and plates were made in considerable quantities. From about 1500 BC onwards additional details were added to the moulded decoration by painting the unfired wares with manganese to give black lines, or by the addition of touches of coloured glass.

(*opposite*) Painted pottery from Egypt (*top*) and Iran (*bottom*).

(*below*) Two cups of *Egyptian faïence* from Egypt, *c.* 1300 BC.

Early glazed earthenware

The alkaline glaze used on 'Egyptian faïence' could not easily be applied to an earthenware body since the contraction of the glaze and body on cooling was so different that the glaze would have peeled. Glazes formed from a mixture of lead and alkalis with quartz were, however, used on late 'Egyptian faïence', and these were suitable for earthenware. The use of glazes only really came to the fore after 1000 BC with the manufacture of the coloured glazed brick reliefs that were amongst the crowning glories of Nineveh and Babylon. The colouring materials were exactly those used to embellish 'Egyptian faïence', and it is interesting to note that, to prevent one colour running into another, motifs were often surrounded by a heavy black line of manganese frit. Despite the truly vast quantities of glazed brick used in the Mesopotamian cities, glazed pottery of this period is rare and most of it very fragmentary. Often only the upper part of each vessel was glazed.

Polychrome glazed bricks. Palace of Darius, Susa, *c.* 500 BC.

Mycenean cup, c. 1300 BC and painted Minoan jar, c. 1400 BC.

Crete and Mycenae

Of the three major types of decorative ware known in the ancient world, painted pottery dominated the Greek world, although the technique of decoration was to undergo drastic changes. Minoan pottery showed considerable variation from small cups of egg-shell thinness to enormous storage jugs as tall as a man, or bathtubs that also served at times as coffins. The larger vessels were normally adorned with relief decoration such as rosettes, but the smaller vessels were commonly painted. The clay of which they were made was clearly very carefully prepared, firing to a pale buff colour, while the designs were executed in a range of ochres and dark magnetite pigments. Motifs, too, were extremely varied. Elaborate geometric patterns derived from plant forms were common and also religious symbols, amongst which was the bull. Sea-creatures were popular, particularly the octopus, the arrangement of whose tentacles allowed the artist great scope. In about 1400 BC the Minoan civilization was eclipsed by that of Mycenae on mainland Greece. For the next two centuries, however, the ceramic traditions of Crete were continued by the Mycenaeans who introduced many of their own motifs, including rather clumsy scenes of everyday life.

GREECE
Geometric pottery

The fall of the Mycenaean civilization in the twelfth century resulted in a severe set-back in the art of pottery manufacture, and the products of the next few generations suffered. Even so, the painted wares never completely vanished, and at the two great pot-making centres, Athens and Corinth, a new style gradually emerged. Early Greek decorative wares made use almost entirely of geometric patterns, amongst which banding and the drawing of concentric circles with a compass are the most obvious. Later the running meander pattern was added and even at this stage an important step had been taken, for the horizontal banding divided the body of the pottery into a series of zones, a system which was to be followed in all decorated Greek pottery. Somewhere about the year 750 BC an Athenian potter whose name is unknown, took yet another important step, filling the zones with scenes depicting humans. His figures were rather like stickmen with triangular torsos; the schemes were very largely mythological, but the human had now been introduced.

(*above*) Early Greek vase with geometric patterns, c. 1200 BC.

(*opposite*) Jug painted with friezes of animal figures. Rhodes. c. 600 BC.

12

'Orientalizing' pottery

Levant, in which decoration depended on many sources, including the lotus and naturalistic animals from Egypt, and sphynxes, griffons and other fabulous creatures from Assyrian and Mesopotamian art. These creatures straggled across the whole surface of the pot, often in a rather ungainly and disorganized manner. The Greeks took over the fabulous beasts from their eastern neighbours, but confined them within the zones already established in their geometric pottery, having no regard for natural scale: griffons, lions, gazelles and geese are all drawn to the same height, the aim being to fill the space rather than to produce a naturalistic picture. Figures and animals were painted first in solid black, and through this layer details were scratched in fine lines to reveal the underlying colour of the body. Finally, further contrast was given to the figures by touches of white or purple-red clay. What distinguished Greek pottery from the vast assembly of 'painted' wares of the Middle East was the discovery, made somewhere around the year 700 BC, of a very effective black glossy slip that had unique properties, shortly to be discussed (see page 15).

(*top*) Modern test-pieces before and after firing (*centre*) typical Greek vessels and (*bottom*) Corinthian black-figure jug and cup.

Greek pottery shapes

Looking at a large collection of ornamental Greek pottery one may forget that they were practical, functional vessels. They are, for example, all provided with sturdy handles. The water pitcher (*hydria*) is made with three handles: two for lifting on to the head, and a third for pouring at table. The positioning of the handles on the drinking cups seems rational only when one realizes that they were intended for use in the recumbent position, and the *krater* seems an ideal shape when one knows that the Greeks habitually mixed their wine with water.

The technique of black 'gloss'

Black 'gloss' as used by the Greeks is not a glaze, nor in the normally accepted sense of the word is it a slip. The material can only be produced from clays that contain a high proportion of the mineral *illite*, an extremely fine-particled material that can be separated from other clay minerals by mixing with water and allowing the coarser clays to settle. The illite clay can then be concentrated and applied like a paint. Greek pottery was initially fired under oxidizing conditions and on reaching its maximum temperature the kiln was closed completely when the whole surface of the clay would have been reduced and thus become black. After a period of cooling the kiln was re-opened to allow oxidation, giving time for the untreated areas to become red, while those covered with 'gloss' remained black. One must admire the Greek potters for their astute observation, which allowed them to develop this system using only the simplest equipment.

Corinthian black-figure wares

The Corinthian potters produced their finest work in the half century following the year 675 BC. The local clay fired to a pale buff colour, which was decorated in black gloss with touches of white and purple-red. Many of their vessels were very small, so that decoration had to be scaled down accordingly, often reaching minute proportions. The usual motifs are birds and animals drawn from 'orientalizing' sources, arranged in friezes, although, more rarely, human figures appear. There is a gaiety about Corinthian decoration and particularly human figures often have the air of caricature.

Early Attic black-figure wares

By the early sixth century Athenian artists were no longer uniquely interested in depicting fabulous beasts, for the human being had taken over as the central focus of design. Large *kraters* of this period often show two or more friezes illustrating some myth or legend, as for example, the famous 'François' vase in the Louvre Museum painted by Klitias around 570 BC. On the whole, however, these large vessels appear rather cluttered, and the decoration overdone. In the drawing of the human figure attention to details of anatomy and to correct proportions began to become very apparent.

Later Attic black-figure wares

To many people the later Attic drinking-cups represent the high point of ancient Greek ceramic art, although in order to meet the enormous export demand, painting was too frequently hasty and bad. Of all the artists of this age Exekias may be seen as one of the most remarkable. His celebrated cup showing Dionysos at sea epitomizes the decoration of this period. In fact, Exekias and his contemporaries had

Attic black-figure cup painted by Exekias and (*opposite*) Attic red-figure vase.

brought painting to a point beyond which it would have been difficult to continue without the whole art becoming static and repetitive, unless some major innovation were introduced.

Red-figure wares

Somewhere in the decade following the year 530 BC an Athenian artist began drawing in his figures with a black gloss background, leaving the figures themselves in the red colour of the body. At first both black and red figures appeared on the same vessels, but soon black-figure wares disappeared totally. The following half-century saw the flourishing of this style of decoration in Athens, which was widely copied elsewhere in the Greek world. Experts have distinguished the work of no less than five hundred painters, and not uncommonly two hundred vessels by the same hand. Much attention was given to human anatomy and to details of drapery, as well as to features of perspective.

White-ground wares

The black- and red-figure decoration was essentially a monochromatic technique. There was, however, one group of pottery which appears to have gone some way in achieving polychromatic effects, used in a more or less naturalistic way. At the very end of the black-figure period there had been a limited production of cups in which the background was painted in white slip, presumably to heighten the contrast. With the general change to red-figure painting a new style evolved in which a number of coloured slips were used in conjunction with the red body of the ware and black gloss. The coloured slips varied from ochre-yellow, through differing shades of red and brown, to purple, all of them depending upon mixtures of coloured clays and ochres. Unfortunately, the slips, particularly the white, were liable to chip and rub in service, and since Greek pottery was designed for use, this was a fatal defect. Nevertheless, a large number of oil jars (*lekthoi*) were made in this style specifically to be buried with the dead or as tomb offerings and show a fine colour balance.

Attic oil jug (lekythos), *c*. 520 BC and (*opposite*) drinking beaker (rhyton), fourth century BC.

Greek 'plastic' wares

The main stream of Greek pottery depended upon wheel-thrown vessels, but some moulded wares were also produced, especially by the East Greeks in Anatolia. The Phrygians in central Anatolia continued the earlier Hittite tradition of making moulded vessels, and it was presumably from this source that the East Greeks acquired the habit. The method of production was reserved almost entirely for the manufacture of small bottles and a form of drinking horn (*rhyton*), characteristically shaped as a human or animal's head. In the forming process slabs of clay were pressed into the halves of a two-piece mould and luted together, handles being applied after moulding. The figures are normally grotesques or caricatures, and one is inclined to feel that the Greeks themselves looked upon them as something of a gimmick. Indeed, Greek 'plastic' wares would have had no place in the history of ceramic development had they not provided an important link between ceramic and metal-working techniques which, in the following centuries, was to prove critical.

ROME
'Megarian' wares

Early in the third century BC the Greeks of southern Italy
resorted to a subterfuge that was to have far-reaching results.
Beginning with an already old silver or bronze repoussé work
bowl, they prepared from it a mould in which they could form
repeated copies, which were then covered with gloss and
fired under reducing conditions. These black Calene bowls
were clearly the product of a pretty shrewd business venture,
for within the century the wares, but not the precise technique, were being copied all over the Mediterranean. Known
centres where these copies were made were in Greece, Syria
and Egypt, although, since the wares were first recognized
at Megara in mainland Greece, they are always referred to as
'Megarian' bowls. The moulds, however, were now no longer
cast directly from existing metal vessels. First a thick-walled
bowl, which itself would be the mould, was thrown on a
wheel. While still damp, reliefs were pressed into the inner
surface of the mould, and further embellishments of running
patterns were added using the edge of a roulette, a small
wheel bearing the design on its rim.

Inner surface of a mould for producing Arretine wares, *c.* 25 BC.
(*opposite*) Megarian bowl with moulded decoration, *c.* 300 BC.

Arretine wares

Megarian wares never really escaped the influence of the
metal vessels from which they took root. The shape was
always basically that of a pudding basin with, or without, an
added foot. The lower part of the vessel usually bore a calyx
of leaves, above which were set groups of human figures,
the stamps for which were not uncommonly made directly
from existing metal vessels. Rouletting was used below the
rim and sometimes as vertical bands to separate the figure
groups. Small stamps bearing the name of the potter were
frequently impressed into the base. Shortly after the middle
of the first century BC a new impetus was given to this type of
ware by the potters of Arezzo. Their products were superior
to the Megarian for a number of reasons: partly because they
were meticulous about the preparation of the clay body, and
partly because it was decided to fire their wares under oxidizing conditions which resulted in a smooth, brilliant, coral-
red surface. Such was the success of Arretine wares that they
were soon to be copied as, for example, at Puteoli near Naples
and at Modena in the north.

21

Samian wares

Samian ware or *terra sigillata*, as it is alternatively known, began to be made in the Toulouse region, particularly at La Graufesenque, shortly before the middle of the first century AD. It was not only a close imitation of Arretine pottery, but in many ways it surpassed it, for the body was made of a stouter fabric, and the gloss surface was even more lustrous, so that it rapidly replaced Arretine. The manufacture of Samian soon spread to other parts of Gaul, to Vichy, and then to the Marne-Rhine region, with an important centre at Lezoux. The products of the latter area are usually easily distinguished from those of La Graufesenque, being yellower and having a less lustrous surface. The high standards of quality and artistic design of the first century AD were not to be maintained, and by the second century one finds wares decorated with rather poorly modelled human figures and animals. By the middle of the third century decoration had become a meaningless scatter of motifs over the surface. Samian pottery began to be copied in North Africa in the second century, but not the technique. The wares were either covered with a thin red slip varying from glossy to matt (Late A Ware), or the surface was burnished as the pots rotated on a

Samian bowl made at La Graufesenque, *c.* 100 AD and (*opposite*) some common forms of Samian ware: bowls, dishes and cups.

wheel (Late B Ware). Their production ceased with the Vandal invasion of 430 AD. Further East, pottery of the same genre was being made in Egypt and Syria, and probably many other centres as well, while in Anatolia its production continued as late as the seventh century.

Typical Samian forms

Like Greek pottery, Samian was made largely for use at table, but unlike the Greek wares very few of the vessels had handles. The most common types were bowls, cups and dishes, and one must suppose that the jugs that were used with them were normally made of metal. Samian ware was, of course, mass-produced. One finds, therefore, the same shapes repeated time and time again. The limited number of forms were first seriously classified by H. Dragendorff in 1895, who allocated a number to each major group of shapes. Since then it has become common practice to refer to Samian vessels by the Dragendorff form number. Over the long period in which Samian was in use shapes remained remarkably stable, and the only reliable criterion of period is the quality of the decoration which became progressively worse with time.

'Marbled' bowl, La Graufesenque, c. 100 AD, and carved beaker, Lezoux c. 200 AD.

Carved and marbled Samian

It would be wrong to give the impression that Samian wares were always decorated in relief or always red. Furthermore, there was a very limited production, perhaps to meet individual demand, of reduced black Samian ware. Two decorative techniques, however, demand especial attention for they show that even in an industry as commercialized as that of Samian manufacture there was room for experimentation. At Graufesenque, in the first century AD, a small quantity of 'marbled' Samian was made. The red body was partly covered with a yellow gloss material, and while still wet this was streaked either by shaking the vessel or with a brush to produce the marbled surface. Again, in the second century at Lezoux, plain shapes were cut with a knife while the vessel was still damp to give leaf-patterns formed by a number of relatively deep facets. Both styles of decoration were short-lived, for they were probably too time-consuming for mass-production, but they do illustrate the impact of contemporary styles in glass manufacture. The marbled wares were clearly an attempt to copy the multicoloured agate glasses then in vogue, while the cut Samian equally clearly echoes the current taste for cut glassware a century later.

Roman slip-trailed wares

One other major system of decoration was used on Samian pottery, that of slip-trailing or *barbotine*. A thick slip of clay was applied through a quill to the damp surface of the wares much as icing sugar may today be used to decorate a cake. Initially, in the first century AD, the technique was used to decorate the rims of otherwise plain dishes, the design normally being a simple repeat leaf pattern. In the second century the system was further developed so that decoration covered the whole surface of a vessel, but apart from using trailed slip, some motifs, such as blossoms, were applied from small individual moulds ('sprig moulds'). This combination of slip-trailing and sprig moulding was used particularly to show hunting scenes incorporating hounds and hares. At Caistor, near Norwich, and at Trier, *barbotine* decoration followed by the application of a thin red slip in imitation of Samian was at first employed, but there followed a highly successful system in which trailed slip in white was applied over a surface that had previously been covered with a thin slip of dark-firing clay, providing a vivid contrast between the vessel and the relief decoration.

Jug, decorated by slip-trailing, the Rhine, *c*. 300 AD.

Roman glazed wares

The glazed wares of the ancient world (see pages 9 and 10) continued to be made in small quantities under the aegis of Rome. From the first century AD at Tarsus and a few other centres in Anatolia a simple lead glaze, made green with copper, was applied to moulded vessels formed of a buff body. The shapes and decoration copied closely those of silver and bronze cups, jugs and bowls, and occasionally decoration was carried out in *barbotine*. By the second century AD very similar wares in a red body were being produced in Europe. Centres of production were at St Rémy-en-Rollet, Vichy, Lezoux, Cologne, Bonn, Denbighshire and Pannonia (modern Hungary). The wares were set in the kiln on stilts, often enclosed in other vessels, 'saggars', which protected the glaze from the soot of the fire. Lead-glazed wares were thus widespread throughout the Roman Empire, but alkaline glazed wares were more limited. A small amount of 'Egyptian faïence' continued to be made in Egypt. In Parthia (southern Mesopotamia), however, quite a different ware was being produced. This was normally wheel-thrown, of a fine white sandy body, and covered with an alkaline glaze similar to that on 'Egyptian faïence'.

Amphora with alkaline glaze, Egypt, and lead-glazed cup, Anatolia, both *c.* 100 AD.

(*opposite*) Jug from Nubia painted in coloured slips, *c.* 200 AD.

Nubian and Nabataean painted wares

In Nabataea, the small Arab state centred around the great caravan centre of Petra, local potters produced a remarkably thin red earthenware painted in lustrous purple-black magnetite. The main output was of bowls which are so thin that they were probably turned after being wheel-thrown. The decorative motifs were derived from those on Hellenistic pottery, but had become highly formalized, usually palm fronds or vines radiating from the centre of the bowl, in which the leaves and bunches of grapes had been reduced to simple geometric forms. To what extent Nabataean pottery continued to be made after the country was annexed by Rome early in the second century AD is a matter of conjecture, but the style of decoration certainly seems to be echoed in that of the early Islamic lustre wares (see page 33). In the upper reaches of the Nile the Nubians also produced a painted ware either on a buff body or a red body covered with a buff slip. The forms were evidently derived from earlier Greek and Roman wares, but the painting embodied elements of both classical and ancient Egyptian art. The latter is to be seen particularly in the treatment of animals and human figures.

CHINA AND ISLAM TO THE TENTH CENTURY
Han lead-glazed wares

With the advent of the Han Dynasty in 206 BC China embarked upon a period of territorial expansion which ultimately brought her outposts into close proximity with those of the Roman Empire. It is apparently from this source that the Chinese learnt to use lead glazes, and it is from this period that the long and complex history of Chinese ceramics really begins. Just as the Late Hellenistic and Roman lead-glazed cups and jars copied quite closely the forms of bronze vessels, so with the Chinese, save that they chose not the Roman but their own splendid bronzes as prototypes to copy. In fact, the materials were ideally suited for this purpose, for the red earthenware body – shaped by pressing into a mould – gave to the lead glaze a green colour not totally dissimilar to that of a well patinated bronze. Not all the Han wares that copied bronze vessels were glazed, however, for there is a considerable group of plain red earthenwares painted in green copper pigments aiming to achieve a similar effect.

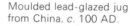

Moulded lead-glazed jug from China, c. 100 AD.

(*opposite*) Wheel-thrown stoneware jug from China, c. 300 AD.

Early Chinese stonewares

Lead glazes were to be short-lived in China. The period following the Han, the Six Dynasties (220–589 AD), was one of great technological innovation in many fields including ceramics, and it is from this period that a form of alkaline glazing took root. The glazes may have been made from the alkalis and silica derived from plant ashes (ash glaze); they may equally have been made from finely crushed felspar; or they may have been made from a mixture of the two. One thing, however, is certain: the kilns in use were capable of higher temperatures than those used for the lead-glazed earthenware, for the body to which the glazes were applied was a dense, heavy stoneware, sometimes quaintly called 'proto-porcelain'. Many of the vessels of this period still show an obsession with metallic prototypes, an influence that was to linger on into the subsequent T'ang period. More typical, however, are the rather heavy stoneware jars, wheel-thrown, with sparse decoration, the upper parts of which are covered with a thin, mottled olive-grey glaze.

Yüeh stoneware bowl with green glaze, *c.* 700 AD.

Yüeh wares

Perhaps during the Six Dynasties, and certainly by early T'ang times (618–906 AD), began the manufacturing of one of the most important groups of Chinese wares made in Chekiang province in eastern China – the Yüeh wares. Made of a stoneware body which is usually grey, but may be oxidized red, the surface is covered with a glaze that varies from olive to grey-green. Typical Yüeh shapes are ewers, jars, dishes and bowls, on which decoration tends to be fairly sparse. Birds, dragons and plant motifs are the usual designs. Apparently rather later than Yüeh was the development of a fine white stoneware, H'sing, that was to all intents a porcelain. Manufactured in Hopei province, from a body made of kaolin mixed with felspar, it was covered with a felspathic glaze that is usually cold and white, sometimes tinged slightly grey or green. Like the Yüeh wares, the decoration is slight. H'sing, however, did not meet with universal approval, especially amongst tea-drinkers. To paraphrase a Chinese commentator: H'sing is like silver, Yüeh is like jade; H'sing is like snow, Yüeh is like ice; H'sing makes tea seem red, Yüeh makes tea seem green; the discriminating choose Yüeh.

T'ang earthenware

Although the T'ang dynasty saw the introduction of true stonewares and porcelain, it also saw the most extraordinary flourishing of lead-glazed earthenware, thereafter to disappear completely from the Chinese scene. In these wares the body was either white, pale buff, or coloured, covered with a white slip. Under the lead glaze the wares were thus essentially white or pale cream, but before the glaze was applied, copper, cobalt and iron pigments were applied to the surface which stained the glaze green, blue and amber. These colours naturally ran into the glaze, and in some cases an attempt was made to prevent this by delimiting the coloured areas with a deep, engraved line. Commonly, however, the colours were applied in an apparently random manner. The moulded reliefs applied to their surfaces would often seem to be little better than poor copies of repoussé work, while the engraved decoration often has precise parallels in chased silver dishes. Even the forms themselves – jugs with sharply defined neck, body and foot; fluted dishes; plates with foliate rims – all suggest an imitation of metal vessels.

T'ang moulded lead-glazed dish with polychrome decoration.

Samarra tin-glazed wares

In 836 AD the Caliphs of Baghdad built a suburban palace at Samarra, and it is from the excavations of this ruin that the story of Islamic pottery begins to unfold. We know that the Abbasid rulers came into direct conflict with the Chinese, whom they defeated in 751 AD, and from Samarra have been recovered fragments of Yüeh and H'sing pottery. It is natural, therefore, to look upon early Islamic glazed wares as attempts to copy Chinese imports, and at least one category seems to fall well within this definition. This group, mostly bowls and dishes, are of a yellow or pink brick body, to the surface of which was applied a lead glaze made white and opaque by the addition of tin. On this surface, decoration was painted in copper, cobalt, manganese and more rarely antimony (yellow), the whole then being covered with a clear lead glaze. The tin glaze may well have been an attempt to emulate H'sing wares, while the underglaze colours seem to echo T'ang earthenware, especially when applied as a 'splash'. On the other hand, some motifs have a more local origin, as for example the half-palmette, which clearly harks back to Hellenistic wares.

Tin-glazed bowl from Mesopotamia, c. 900 AD.

Multi-coloured lustre dish from Mesopotamia, *c.* 900 AD.

Early lustre wares

A second group of early Islamic wares seem to owe nothing at all to Chinese influence. These are of a closely grained grey or buff earthenware which was first covered with a clear lead glaze and then fired. To this surface were applied mixtures containing copper and silver salts and sulphur, which when fired again under heavily reducing conditions, produced a metallic lustre. The colour of the lustre varied according to the mixture, and early lustre wares showed the use of two or more contrasting colours, a practice soon to be abandoned in favour of a single colour. The technique appears to have been derived from a comparable method of producing lustres on glass, evolved in Egypt at about the same period, but the motifs employed, and the rather delicate brush-work used, seem to derive from yet another source. The motifs are largely either formalized leaf patterns or animal and, more rarely, human figures. The floral patterns seem to echo quite closely those used on Nabataean wares, while the human and animal figures often resemble Nubian and Coptic painted wares.

Sgraffiato wares

A third major group of early Islamic pottery is of a plain, red earthenware body which was covered with a white slip. While still damp, a pattern was scratched through the slip to reveal the underlying body. The whole surface was then covered with a clear lead glaze. These wares are now generally known as 'sgraffiato', a term borrowed from the writing of the Italian potter, Piccolpasso (see page 73), and which literally means 'scratched'. Early sgraffiato bowls and dishes show a strong resemblance to metalwork, the designs being largely of a geometric character, and the lead glaze being without additional colour. By the tenth century, however, green (copper), purple (manganese), brown and ochre (iron) began to be used under the glaze, while designs began to incorporate human and animal figures. Often the colours were applied in a manner totally unrelated to the sgraffiato design, but were occasionally used to fill in solid areas contained by the lines of decoration. Even so, the colours normally ran into the glaze. Although the sgraffiato wares initially show a strong resemblance to contemporary metalwork, there seems to be some attempt to copy the overall appearance of Yüeh pottery.

Samarquand slip-painted wares

By the tenth century yet a fourth major system of decoration had been developed in Persia and Turkestan, in which an attempt was made to prevent colours running in the glaze. A slip was first applied over an earthenware body which might be red (Samarquand) or buff (Persia). Over this were painted other slips coloured purple (manganese), green (copper) or tomato red (iron), each area being delimited by a fine line drawn with a pointed tool. At times the whole surface was covered with a coloured slip, and the decoration picked out in white. The whole was then covered with a clear lead glaze. The vessels were normally bowls, plates and dishes. Early examples of these wares were decorated with palmettes, and very commonly with an inscription in Cufic script, usually a blessing upon the user, around the edge. Later, birds, animals and human beings became common motifs, particularly on wares made in the Sari area, southeast of the Caspian Sea. In vessels made in the Nishapur region of north Persia the coloured areas were outlined in a pigment containing a large quantity of manganese, deep purple or black, which very effectively prevented the other colours running in the glaze.

Slip-painted dishes and (*opposite*) *sgraffiato* bowl with splashed decoration in colour, all three Nishapur, *c.* 900 AD.

CHINA AND ISLAM TO THE THIRTEENTH CENTURY

T'ang and Sung forms

To many students of pottery the Sung dynasty (960–1260) saw the flowering of Chinese ceramics. We saw earlier how many of the T'ang shapes adhered pretty closely to the metal prototypes from which they were copied. During the Sung period these same basic forms were very considerably modified better to suit being thrown on the wheel. Profiles, which during the T'ang period had been angled at neck and base, now became a continuous sweeping curve; bowls became fuller and more rounded; while handles – never a predominant feature of T'ang wares – now tended to disappear. Briefly, the clay body had become a material in its own right, and vessel forms were developed that suited the potter's craft, utmost simplicity of shape being the keynote of the period.

Typical T'ang (*left*) and Sung (*right*) forms.

Lung-ch'üan celadon

From the tenth century onwards there began in China the manufacture of a varied group of wares generically known as 'celadons', a European term, said to have been derived from the name of the hero of the seventeenth-century French romance, *l'Astrée*, in which he wore a costume of grey-green. The early celadons, the Lung-ch'üan, made in Southern Chekiang province (south-east China) clearly owed a great deal to the earlier Yüeh wares. The body is a greyish-white stoneware, which may be saffron when oxidized, but which in hardness and composition approaches porcelain. The glaze, which was more viscous than that of Yüeh, varies in colour from leaf-green to a cold blue-green or sea-green. The glaze, like that of Yüeh ware, certainly contained plant ash and felspar. Decoration was normally lightly carved in the body before glazing, more rarely moulded, and in general was confined to plant motifs. One group of Lung-ch'üan celadons with a glaze that is bluer than the normal types has been greatly prized, especially by Japanese collectors.

Celadon bowl of Lung-ch'üan type. *c.* 1100 AD.

Northern celadon

The production of the so-called 'northern celadons' began at
much the same time as did the Lung-ch'üan wares, the chief
centres of manufacture being at Yao-chou in Shensi province
and at Lin-ju in central Honan. These wares were also clearly
derived from Yüeh. Usually they have a brown-buff stoneware body, again approaching porcelain in hardness, over
which was applied an olive-green glaze of much the same type
as on Lung-ch'üan wares, but more lustrous. Exuberant
decoration was carved – and more rarely moulded – into the
body before the application of the glaze. Flower patterns
were the most common motifs, of which the peony, highly
formalized, was evidently a favourite. Early Chinese writers
refer to Tung-ching (or Tung ch'ing) wares, a term translated
to mean Eastern Capital (or green) wares. Both the Lung-
ch'üan and northern celadons became articles of extensive
trade, and by the thirteenth century decoration had become
more flamboyant to meet, one feels, the demands of this
market. But in China the tastes of the ruling classes followed
a very different set of aesthetic values, (see page 39).

Ju and Kuan wares

Early in the twelfth century kilns were set up in Kaifong specifically to serve the Imperial household. The pottery, known as Ju ware, was a soft pinkish-buff stoneware body covered with a thick luminous glaze, smooth and dense, varying from lavender to greenish-blue in colour. Shapes were simple, even austere, and decoration, carried out by carving under the glaze, was minimal. The earliest known test-piece of Ju ware is dated 1107. By 1127 the Chinese rulers, as a result of Tartar invasions, were forced to move their capital south to Hangchow, when the production of Ju wares ceased. The kilns were working for only a matter of some twenty years, but by 1130 new kilns had been set up in the palace grounds when the manufacture of Kuan (Imperial or Official) wares began. Made of a thin, dark-grey stoneware body, the pottery was covered with a glaze that varies from lavender to blue-green or even a creamy ash-grey. Shape and decoration followed very much that of the Ju wares. Essentially both Ju and Kuan glazes were of the celadon family and both tend to crackle heavily, Kuan more so than Ju. While not aesthetically unpleasant, and even admired by some, the crackle probably results from the heavy application of glaze.

Bowl of Ju ware and plate of Kuan ware, both c. 1100 AD and (opposite) bowl of 'northern' celadon, c. 1100 AD.

Chün wares

Chün wares may well have been an early off-shoot of the general celadon family, having many features in common with the celadons, Ju and Kuan wares. They were made at several localities in Honan province of a rather soft grey or buff body. The glaze is thick and opalescent, having been applied as several coatings. The glaze material contained a considerable proportion of plant ash, and although it may be grey-green or blue-green, it is more commonly a lavender blue. Carved or moulded decoration is extremely scant. So far, in fact, a verbal description of Chün pottery differs little from that of the Ju or Kuan wares. Very frequently, however, Chün vessels are decorated with 'splashes' of vivid purple-red resulting from applying spots of copper salts at a late stage in the glazing process and firing under reducing conditions. This is a difficult technique to perfect, but so much did it attract later Chinese craftsmen, that many of the Chün vessels in collections are later successful copies. It is hard to say what prompted this development, for it seems to have no antecedents, and reduced copper glazes (*sang-de-boeuf*) did not come into general use until a much later period.

Honan black stonewares

During the Sung period a wide range of stonewares with black glazes was also manufactured. The bodies were white (Honan) or grey (Chien in Fukien), and on rare occasions the black glaze was applied to true porcelain bodies. The glaze material itself was an ash or felspar composition containing a high proportion of iron which, like the celadons, was fired under reducing conditions. Although referred to as black glazes, the colours are often very deep browns, and into the glaze was frequently introduced a variety of pattern effects most of which depended upon 'resist' methods, in which areas of the surface were either free of the dark glaze material or it was effected by some previous treatment. In the so-called 'oil-spot' decoration the surface is patterned with a spatter of iridescent spots. The surface was clearly treated with some material which modified the glaze. The same must be true of the 'hare's fur' markings which show fine striations in the glaze radiating from a central point, in character not very different from 'mocha' ware (see page 139).

Honan black stonewares with reserve decoration (jug) and oil-spot decoration (bowl), both c. 1100 AD and (opposite) Chün ware plate and water-dropper, both c. 1100 AD.

Tz'u-chou monochrome slip-painted wares

The Tz'u-chou stonewares represent a completely different tradition in Chinese ceramics. Normally they are profusely decorated and heavily potted of a buff or greyish body, as would have been suitable for the wine and storage jars, basins and other domestic vessels which largely comprise this group of wares. The manufacture of Tz'u-chou wares was widespread in China, although the name derives from a town in Northern Honan province. Two principal techniques of decoration were used: underglaze slip-painting and *sgraffiato* work. Often the stoneware body was first covered with a white slip which frequently stopped short of the foot of the vessel, and on to this surface was painted the decoration in black or brown slip: sometimes this situation was reversed. These black and white slip-painted wares are quite remarkable for the deft, free-handling of the brush, which is both bold and surprisingly economic. The normal motifs are leaf and flower patterns, admirably suited to this type of work. Although a clear glaze was at first used, in late Sung and subsequent periods the glaze was occasionally coloured blue (cobalt) or turquoise (copper).

Stoneware slip-painted vase of Tz'u-chou type, *c*. 1100 AD.

Tz'u-chou polychrome slip-painted wares

The most dramatic Tz'u-chou slip-painted wares are un-doubtedly the monochromes, but polychrome vessels were also manufactured. A small but important group of such wares was made as early as the Liao period (907–1255 AD) in Man-churia, and it is probably from this source that Tz'u-chou slip-painting was derived. The Liao vessels, however, lack the free-hand painting of the later Tz'u-chou, each area of slip being carefully delimited by a neatly scored line. The decoration of formalized flower motifs was executed on a white slip using green (copper), yellow and red (iron) and more rarely black (manganese). It was not until the thirteenth century that this system was replaced by the use of pre-formed coloured glaze (frits) applied at a second (glost) firing on the already glazed wares. Clearly the Tz'u-chou and Samarquand slip-painted wares (see page 35) have so much technically in common that they must be related. This is less surprising when one realizes that the two areas were far from isolated, for they were connected by the Great Silk Road, along which many traders were conducting their business.

Stoneware bowl with polychrome slip-painting. *c.* 1100 AD.

Stoneware jars decorated with *sgraffiato* under clear and coloured glazes, *c.* 1100 AD.

Tz'u-chou *sgraffiato* wares

The second major method of decoration used on Tz'u-chou wares, *sgraffiato*, was identical in general technique to that developed in the Middle East (see page 34), although it must be pointed out that the Islamic pottery was earthenware, while the Chinese was stoneware: the former covered with a lead glaze, the latter with an alkaline one. Furthermore in the Tz'u-chou wares both motifs and the precise method of cutting through the white slip were specifically Chinese. The main motifs employed were formalized flower patterns, while one of the principal engraving tools was of bamboo, and it is not uncommon to find the backgrounding to the flower patterns carried out by cutting through the slip with the hollow end of a bamboo stick, to provide an effect somewhat similar to that used as a background in some classes of metalwork. Thus the Tz'u-chou wares may well echo some aspects of contemporary local metalwork.

Tz'u-chou: carved *sgraffiato* wares

An extension of the *sgraffiato* technique appears in the so-called Tz'u-chou carved wares. Stoneware decorated in this style was first covered with a slip, as in other *sgraffiato* wares, but instead of employing a simple linear decoration, large expanses were cut away to reveal the underlying body. The common motifs found on carved *sgraffiato* wares were based on flowers such as the peony and chrysanthemum. Although a colourless glaze might be used, it became a common practice to colour the clear glaze green (copper) and more rarely blue (cobalt), a style of decoration paralleled in the later Tz'u-chou monochrome slip-painted wares (see page 42). In such cases the combination of colouring materials, derived from both glaze and body, made the areas that had been cut away appear almost black, an effect heightened by the fact that the glaze tended to 'pool' in the recessed areas. To what extent these wares influenced, or were influenced by, the contemporaneous 'Garrus' pottery of northern Persia (see page 49) is a matter of conjecture, but in view of the other known technological parallels between the East and West during this period, one must again assume that the two developments were not entirely isolated.

Ting porcelain jar and plate, both
c. 1200 AD.

Ting and Ying-ch'ing

The Sung period also saw the introduction of true porcelain,
quantities of which were exported to the West. These wares
had such an impact on the rest of the Old World that, although
they do not come within the compass of this book, a word
should be said about them here. The finest of the Sung
porcelain, Ting ware, has a greyish-white body and was
covered with a thin warm ivory glaze, free of crazing but
often containing bubbles. Decoration, similar in character
to that on the celadons, was carved or moulded into the underlying body. They were turned on the undecorated surface,
while in the green-hard state, to make them thinner. After
the application of the liquid glaze material, the vessels were
stood upright to dry so that the glaze tended to weep, leaving
the rims almost bare of glaze and thick tears around the bases.
The other important type of porcelain produced during the
Sung period has a white, translucent, sugary body and is
covered with a glaze that varies from pale blue to pale green,
sometimes with ferruginous spots. These wares are known
by dealers as Ying-ch'ing (misty blue) or as Ch'ing-pai.

Seljuk carved wares

The presence of the Seljuks in the Islamic world was to stimulate trade with the Far East, putting new demands upon the local potters. The demand for porcelain was so great that a completely new type of body was created to fill the gap: or, to be more precise, an old type of ware was resurrected. The glaze was made by fusing quartz pebbles and potash which was reduced to a fine powder (frit) and mixed with water before application. The body was made of ten parts of powdered quartz, one part of white plastic clay and one part of the same frit as used for the glaze. In composition, therefore, the materials were similar to those used in the manufacture of Egyptian faïence (see page 9), and identical to the Roman alkaline glazed wares (see page 26). To complete the imitation of Ting and Ying-ch'ing imported wares, decoration on the Seljuk white vessels was carved into the underlying body, the clear glaze tending to pool into the deep recesses of the carving. Theoretically the glaze should have adhered adequately, but in fact the glaze frit was not as good as it should have been, and in some examples one sees today it has peeled off completely.

'Seljuk' dish in carved white ware with coloured glaze, Persia, c. 1150 AD.

Seljuk moulded wares

The Seljuk white body was to prove to be no flash-in-the-pan as a development, and from the beginning of the twelfth century onwards the composition was to be used more and more for the production of fine wares in Persia and other Islamic countries. In the latter half of the twelfth century Persian craftsmen took to using blue and green glazes and to moulding their vessels. The moulds were made of two opposing pieces into which slabs of material were pressed. The mould pieces were then put together and the junction smoothed over on the inside. On the outer surface the junction lines were more carefully fettled, but seldom with sufficient care to obscure them completely. Indeed, there are so many signs of shoddy work that one can only assume that demand had far outrun production. The moulded designs, largely leaves and flower patterns, became stereotyped and perfunctory, so that by the thirteenth century these wares were well on the way to becoming a bad peasant craft and had reached such a low ebb, that after the Mongol invasion of the thirteenth century they were never to be rejuvenated.

'Seljuk' moulded jug, Persia, *c.* 1300 AD and (*opposite*) 'Garrus' *sgraffiato* plate, Persia, *c.* 1200 AD.

'Garrus' *sgraffiato* wares

During the eleventh and twelfth centuries *sgraffiato* decoration (see page 34) became widespread in the Islamic world, and a number of quite distinct regional 'schools' developed. The so-called 'Amol' wares are of a simple scratched design covered with a clear or uniformly coloured glaze, while in the later products there was a tendency to emphasize the lines by filling them with a green (copper) pigment before glazing. The 'Aghkand' wares were also initially carried out in simple linear *sgraffiato*, but areas enclosed by the lines were coloured green (copper), yellow (antimony), or purple (manganese) before glazing. The *sgraffiato* lines were intended to prevent the colours from running in the glaze. The most interesting group of *sgraffiato* wares of this period are, however, the so-called 'Garrus' or 'Champlevé' type. In these, as with the carved *sgraffiato* Tz'u-chou (see page 45), whole areas of the initial slip were cut away to provide a strong contrast between the slip and underlying body. The usual motifs were animals, scrolls and Cufic inscriptions, often covered with a coloured glaze.

Lakabi wares

The twelfth century saw the introduction in Persia of white wares with underglaze polychrome colouring. The 'Lakabi' wares (the word simply means 'coloured') where made of the white quartz-frit body developed for Seljuk pottery into which designs were either carved or moulded. Areas were then coloured with blue (cobalt), yellow (antimony), purple (manganese) or green (copper) pigments, and the whole surface covered with a clear glaze. Pottery of this type was produced in the great Persian caravan centres of Kashan and Rayy (Rhages), for only a limited period, in the middle to late twelfth century. It cannot have been looked upon as an unqualified success despite its rustic charm, but it does illustrate the effect that contemporary Persian miniature painting was beginning to have upon ceramics. There was clearly a demand for complete polychromy set against a white background. The importance of Lakabi wares, historically, lies in the fact that they represent the turning-point in ceramic taste.

Moulded Lakabi dish with polychrome colouring, *c.* 1200 AD.

'Minai' or 'Haft rang' wares

In the late twelfth and early thirteenth centuries Persian craftsmen rapidly evolved a system for producing full polychromy. The wares, known as 'Minai' (enamelled) or 'Haft rang' (seven colours), demanded two distinct firings. The wares were first decorated with the underglaze colours, blue (cobalt), purple (manganese) and green (copper), were then covered with glaze, and fired. The remaining colours, prepared low-temperature frits, were then painted over the glaze and the wares were fired again to a temperature sufficient only to fuse the frits. These 'enamel' colours were black (a mixed pigment containing manganese), browns and reds (derived from ferruginous clays) and white (tin). Touches of leaf gilding completed the range. The favourite motifs on these wares were 'lifted', almost without modification, from Persian miniature painting – horsemen, court ladies, hunting scenes, and so on. The technique, however, was apparently too demanding, and the earliest wares produced at Rayy, prior to its sack by Mongols in 1224, were undoubtedly the best.

Polychrome bowl of Minai or Haft rang type, Persia, *c.* 1200 AD.

ISLAM AND BYZANTIUM
Persian underglaze painted wares

According to Abul Qasim by 1300 the production of Minai wares had ceased, although insipid enamelling (Lajvard) in black, brown, red and white, often on a cobalt blue glaze, continued for a short period. Parallel with the development of fully polychromatic wares, however, the Persian craftsmen had continued with the tradition of underglaze painting in coloured slips (see page 35), and by the early twelfth century had so improved upon their technique, that slip-painted areas were now seldom delimited by a scored line but put on by free-hand painting. Combinations of two or more colours were commonly used under a clear glaze throughout the twelfth and early thirteenth centuries, the common motifs being scrolls, arabesques, figures and plant designs. The main centres of production appear to have been Rayy and Kashan, and from the latter area come a number of dishes with inscriptions, often including the date of manufacture (see page 77). One particularly attractive type of underglaze painted ware depended entirely upon the use of a black slip, the vessels being covered with a blue (cobalt) or turquoise (copper) glaze.

Byzantine underglaze painted wares

In Byzantium, from the ninth century onwards, one finds lead glazes more and more commonly in use, parallel with development of Islamic glazed wares. In Corinth, at much the same time, undecorated wares, made of local buff clay (see page 14), were covered with a lead glaze which fired a lemon yellow. By the tenth century Byzantine potters had begun to experiment with underglaze painting, often leaving the undecorated areas of the surface bare of glaze. Following the Seljuk invasion of Anatolia, in the latter part of the eleventh century, however, the quality of these polychrome wares declined abruptly, and throughout the twelfth century the larger part of Byzantine polychrome pottery is best seen as a poor copy of current Persian wares. Common motifs were animals, birds and figures roughly outlined in black (manganese), blocked in with green, blue and brown, set against a white background. Much of this decoration was carried out not on a white bodied ware, but on red earthenware covered with a white slip.

Byzantine underglaze painted plates from Corinth and Byzantium, *c.* 1300 AD and (*opposite*) Persian underglaze painted plate, *c.* 1300 AD.

Persian and Syrian *sgraffiato* wares

We have already seen how Islamic *sgraffiato* wares developed in Persia (see page 49) to produce a number of regional variants. It would be wrong, however, to think that these were the only centres of production, even if they were to set the fashion. Local variants were being produced at a number of centres throughout Islam, and for the moment those wares produced in Northern Mesopotamia and Syria must demand attention, for it was from the Levant coast that, intermittently throughout the twelfth century, the Crusaders learnt directly of Islamic pottery. From the ruins of the port of Al Mina (St Symeon), and a number of Crusaders' castles, have been recovered quantities of polychrome and *sgraffiato* wares. They are remarkable not for their technique, for in fact their making shows little skill, but for the mixed nature of their decoration. Thus some of the dishes portray birds and animals, and these could have been manufactured to suit Islamic tastes; others, however, depict knights in fighting array, and more rarely, coats-of-arms. Such wares must have been made for the Crusaders. Apart from the rather yellow lead glaze covering the white slip, green (copper) and brown (iron) were used, probably in imitation of the 'Aghkand' wares (see page 49), to colour areas of the surface.

Byzantine *sgraffiato* wares

From the ninth century onwards Byzantine potters had experimented with *sgraffiato* wares as had the Islamic craftsmen (see page 34), and by the eleventh century there was a considerable production of simple *sgraffiato* designs under a clear lead glaze. The favourite motifs were fantastic animals and legendary figures. By the twelfth century, however, the impact of Persian and Syrian *sgraffiato* wares was being felt, when greens and browns began to be used to colour areas of the glaze. By the end of the century it had become quite a common practice to cut away whole areas of slip to reveal the underlying body, clearly in imitation of the 'Garrus' wares of Persia (see page 49). The centres of production were widely spread throughout the Byzantine Empire – Corinth, Salonika and Cyprus were all producing their own variants by the thirteenth century. It must have been largely through Venetian imports from Byzantium and the Levant coast that the people of North and Central Italy first learnt of, and later copied, both the underglaze painted (see page 66) and *sgraffiato* (see page 120) wares.

Byzantine *sgraffiato* bowl and plate, perhaps Salonika, *c.* 1300 AD and (*opposite*) Syrian *sgraffiato* plate with splashed decoration, *c.* 1300 AD.

MEDIEVAL EUROPE
Early European lead-glazed wares

By the ninth century the potter's wheel had been adopted by most European craftsmen, and it is very common to find vessels that were thrown on the wheel, the flat bases of which were then pushed out to give a rounded base suitable for their fires. Unlike the large Roman potteries the medieval craftsmen normally supplied only a local market, and their wares were therefore many and varied. By the tenth century the Vikings had re-opened the sea-routes between Northern Europe and the Mediterranean, and it was probably in imitation of current Byzantine pottery (see page 53) that craftsmen in Hamburg and Stamford, Lincolnshire, began to manufacture jugs and cooking-pots of a pale buff body covered on the outside with a clear, pale yellow, lead glaze, thus re-introducing glazed wares into Northern Europe. It was, however, only the process of glazing that was adopted, and the simple cooking-pots and jugs to which it was applied were essentially of local character.

Lead glazed jug in Stamford ware *c*. 1000 AD. (*opposite*) Lead glazed jugs with coloured slip (*left*) and applied (*right*) decorations.

Medieval wares with slip and applied decoration

In the ninth century at Pingsdorf, near Bonn, there was a thriving production of pale buff wares which, although unglazed, were decorated with a thin red ochreous slip, painted on as dots, circles and waves in broad strokes of the brush. This style of decoration was widely copied, ultimately to form the basis of a range of wares painted in underglaze slips. The same period saw the introduction of copper (green) glazes used all over a surface. A further extension of this scheme of decoration is to be seen in the use of heavily trailed slips and applied bands, dots and rosettes of clay, normally laid on as purely geometric patterns. Thus the potters of Rouen were, by the twelfth century, making jugs of a fine, pale buff body decorated with lines and dots of red clay under a coating of clear lead glaze. During this period the jug was virtually the only ceramic article in table use; dishes, plates and cups were of wood or metal, and it is perhaps for this more than any other reason, that the development of pottery in Northern Europe took its own parochial line of evolution almost divorced from the Byzantine and Islamic worlds in which dishes and bowls played so large a part.

Lead glazed jug with elaborate decoration. Nottingham, c. 1300. (*opposite*) Underglaze painted jug from Saintonge (*left*), c. 1300 AD: and English jug with polychrome applied decoration, c. 1350.

Medieval 'plastic' wares

The late twelfth and early thirteenth centuries saw the climax of the insular development of medieval pottery in England. The jug, which had initially been little more than a cooking-pot with added spout and handles, had by stages become a tall vessel with distinct neck and a single broad handle stretching from the rim to the shoulder of its body. At first crude masks were modelled below the spout, and in turn there appeared, especially from the workshops of Nottingham, a series of jugs with figures modelled in full or low reliefs set around the neck and upper part of the body. The motifs were either groups of knights on horseback or of mounted huntsmen with their hounds chasing deer, the whole surface being covered with a green (copper) glaze. The modelling on these vessels is poor, and had not a sufficiently large number of jugs been found, one might suspect them to be joke-pieces made by a single potter.

Medieval polychrome wares

A taste for polychrome wares began to be felt in Northern Europe in the late thirteenth century. In the twelfth century the potters of Saintes had been making jugs of an almost white body covered with lead glaze. To these were now added decoration in underglaze pigments; designs outlined in black (manganese) with infilled areas of green (copper) and ochre (iron). These wares were technically akin to contemporary pottery in Italy (see page 66) and Spain (see page 62), in turn derived from Byzantium and Islam. Motifs included leaves and half palmettes (see page 32), birds and coats-of-arms (see page 54). Jugs of Saintonge ware were traded with the Bordeaux wines as far afield as Holland and the Scandinavian countries, but in the greatest quantity to England. The English also began to make polychrome jugs of a buff body to which were applied designs based on bands and rosettes. Normally the rosettes were sprig-moulded in a red-firing clay, while the bands were of the same clay as the body, rouletted (see page 20), and tinted green with copper, a clear lead-glaze being applied overall.

SPAIN: HISPANO-MORESQUE WARES
Later Islamic lustre wares

With the collapse of the Fatimid Caliphate (AD 1171) there seems to have been an exodus of craftsmen from Egypt to Persia with the result that there was a sudden flourishing of the manufacture of lustre wares. By the late twelfth century they were being made at Rayy, Rakka and Kashan, and possibly elsewhere in Persia and Syria. The lustre, however, was no longer applied to a red earthenware body, but normally to a white one of the 'Seljuk' type (see page 47), although the Rayy wares can be distinguished by their poor quality and rather pink body. Human figures, often mounted on horses, birds and animals, were the favourite motifs, set against a background of scrolls and arabesques. Lustre was frequently used for backgrounds, leaving the figures in clear white. The potters of Rayy tended particularly towards large figures occupying the greater part of the decorated surface, often surrounded by 'contour' lines but in the Rakka and Kashan workshops groups of figures in the 'Minai' style (see page 51) were more common. The manufacture of lustre wares was, however, to receive a severe blow in the thirteenth century. In 1224 Rayy was

Egyptian lustreware bowl (*left*), and Persian lustreware dish, Kashan, both *c*. 1200.

(*opposite*) Dish of Málaga lustreware, *c*. 1300.

sacked by the Mongols, and Rakka in 1259: only the workshops of Kashan survived.

Málaga lustre wares

Suddenly, in the mid-thirteenth century, there was a great flourishing of lustre manufacture, probably due to the arrival of refugees from Rakka and Rayy who brought the secret of its making with them. The centre of its manufacture was at Málaga in Andalusia, and by the end of the century its exports were going as far afield as Egypt and England. The main output was of bowls, dishes and jugs, all typically 'Persian' in form as, too, were the figure and arabesque designs. Málaga lustre was applied not to a white body, but to a red earthenware previously covered with white tin glaze. The Málaga potters were capable of making very large vessels as, for example, the wing-handled vases in the Alhambra Palace which stand four feet tall, and were made by joining together a number of sections. A large part of the Málaga potteries' production went into the manufacture of decorated tiles, a few of which may still be seen *in situ* in the Alhambra Palace.

Polychrome dishes from
Paterna (*left*) and Teruel
(*right*), both *c*. 1300.
(*opposite*) Lustreware bowl
from Manises, *c*. 1430.

Paterna and Teruel polychrome wares

In the Christian Kingdoms of Castille and Aragon, in the
thirteenth century, a type of pottery was being made which
was technically identical to that of Saintonge (see page 59).
The main centres of production were at Paterna in Valencia and
Teruel in Aragon and the products of the two cities are so
similar that it is often impossible to distinguish them. Jugs,
bowls and dishes were made of a near-white body decorated
in black or purple outlines (manganese) blocked in with green
(copper) and, less commonly, ochre, the whole being covered
with clear lead glaze. The usual motifs were heraldic shields,
animals, knights and dancers. The influence the Islamic
potters exerted was enormous, and the outcome, a blend of
Gothic and Islamic traditions, was to result in one of the most
remarkable groups of pottery to be seen in Western Europe,
the so-called Hispano-Moresque wares. The contribution of
the Moorish potters was so strong that, along with the
arabesque and geometric patterns of Islam, are to be found
Cufic and mock-Cufic inscriptions in lustre on dishes destined
for the use of Christian nobles.

Manises

At first, in about 1400, the Manises potters were content to copy the products of Málaga, so much so that it is difficult to tell the two apart. As they assimilated the features of Gothic design, however, a fresh and quite distinct style emerged. The wares, made of red earthenware body with a lead-tin glaze, were decorated very largely in underglaze cobalt blue and a gold-coloured lustre. The main output was tableware destined for the noble families: bowls, plates, dishes and jugs, as well as drug-jars of typically Islamic form, made often to meet a specific order. By the middle of the fifteenth century Manises pottery was being made for Italian noble families such as the Medici and Gondi. As might be expected with such a clientele, decorative motifs tended to be either coats-of-arms or heraldic beasts. Many dishes were decorated on both surfaces, the whole of the underside often being covered with a single heraldic beast in lustre.

Maiolica

The one single feature that distinguishes the Manises lustre ware from all that came before and most of that which was to follow is the manner in which the painters handled the brush. Capable of minute detail-painting, the potters were equally competent to carry out a design in a few bold, sweeping strokes. Most critics, indeed, agree that such brushwork has never been surpassed in the West. Naturally, the potters of other parts of Spain attempted to emulate the Manises lustre wares, as for example at Teruel, Talavera de la Reina in Toledo and at Barcelona. The technique of manufacture was identical, although slight differences of glaze and lustre colour help to distinguish the products of the various centres. With the passing of the fifteenth century designs of purely Islamic origin became less and less used, and representational drawing more common, perhaps to meet a growing market that was now no longer exclusively of noblemen. Indeed, throughout the second half of the fifteenth century Spanish lustre ware had become an item of very considerable trade. Italian merchants

The face (*left*) and back (*right*) of a dish from Manises, *c*. 1450.

who were in the habit of buying consignments in Majorca shipped the wares back to Italy where they became known generically as 'Maiolica' (see page 71).

Seville: the 'Cuerda seca' technique

In Seville a type of pottery was produced in which an attempt was made to overcome the age-old problem of colours running in the glaze. Around each area of colour was drawn a heavy line in a mixture of manganese and grease which, after firing, left a black unglazed line. This technique, known as *cuerda seca* (dry cord), was not new to Spain. A limited quantity of such wares had been made in Moorish Cordoba from the eleventh century. The *cuerda seca* pottery was of red earthenware which was inclined to be rather heavy. On the whole, motifs tended to be greatly simplified versions of those used on Manises ware, but by comparison the drawing was inept and clumsy. Early in the sixteenth century the process was replaced at Seville by one in which plates and dishes were pressed into a mould so designed, that areas to be glazed were left as depressions separated by raised lines that would remain bare of glaze.

Polychrome dish from Seville in the 'cuerda seca' technique, *c.* 1550.

ITALIAN TIN-GLAZED WARES
Italian late medieval wares

By the mid-thirteenth century Italian potters began to experiment with *sgraffiato* (see page 120) and polychrome wares. By the end of the thirteenth century there were many small workshops scattered throughout the whole country producing a wide variety of wares, but in which the use of underglaze green (copper), purple-black (manganese), and less commonly, cobalt blue on a white ground, are a common feature. Normally the wares were of a pale buff or white body on which motifs were outlined in black and blocked in with green or blue, a technique identical to that in use at Saintes (see page 59) and Paterna (see page 62). The usual vessels were bowls, dishes, jugs and drug-jars, the latter often being bulbous pots with a pair of strap-handles, one set on each side of the body.

Early tin-glazed wares

From about 1425 onwards the use of a tin glaze painted in polychrome became a universal practice throughout Italy. Although there were many centres of pottery production, in the mid-fifteenth century Florence largely set the pace. New colours were introduced: a cobalt frit, *zaffre* – first imported from Syria – potters initially found difficult to handle, so that it appeared as a dark blue impasto under the glaze. Thus for about a quarter of a century there were two main schools of decoration. The first (*la famiglia verde*) adhering to the old palette, predominantly green (copper) and purple (manganese) with touches of ochre; the other (*zaffera in rilievo*) using cobalt frit impasto, usually with touches of purple. Armorial beasts and emblems drawn on a grand scale were frequently surrounded by a pattern of oak leaves, but Islamic features such as the half-palmette and contour lines were also introduced. By the middle of the century large portrait heads and figures began to be used. A rich orange (ochre) and a vivid yellow (antimony) were supplemented by a turquoise derived from an alkaline frit coloured with copper.

Drug-jar and dish. Florence, both *c*. 1450 and (*opposite*) jug, Florence, *c*. 1400. Dish, Orvieto, *c*. 1450.

Faenza

The potters of the Faenza school set in motion a number of
trends, each of which was to be expanded upon in the early
sixteenth century. Individual motifs were borrowed from
elsewhere, as for example, a peacock's feather pattern from
Iznik (see page 79) and vine scrolls from Manises (see page 63),
but an even more important source of inspiration lay in the
printed book. Woodcuts and engravings by such artists as
Schongauer (b. 1446) and Dürer (b. 1471) were adapted as the
central motif, around which were set a pattern embodying a
mixture of Gothic, Persian, Iznik and Hispano-Moresque floral
designs. At the end of the century the potters began to
assimilate features of Renaissance design, as for example
candelabra, grotesque animals and acanthus leaf patterns. At
the same time plates and dishes became less and less functional
and increasingly a feature of architecture or interior decoration, so much so, that they were produced already drilled with
a suspension hole. To some extent the architectural use of
polychrome earthenware had been anticipated by Luca della
Robbia (b.1400) and his son Andrea (b.1437).

The 'fresco' technique

Fresco painting shares so much in common with the decoration of matt tin glaze that potters naturally adopted many of the painters' techniques. In both cases errors in drawing or painting are almost impossible to rectify, and for this reason pounces, or cartoons of pricked lines through which a pigment could be dusted to give an outline of the design, were frequently used. The painters' habit of mixing on the palette was now copied, as, too, was the art of overlaying one colour with another, giving not only a greater possible range of colours, but also allowing shading to give a depth to pictures. In brief, after the turn of the fifteenth century ceramic decoration at times became little more than a miniature fresco. Inevitably decorators turned more and more to painters for their inspiration, and their work is often no more than a copy of a painting by such artists as Perugino, Botticelli or Donatello. To complete the parallel, it became common practice to cover these highly decorated wares with a final coat of clear lead glaze, *coperta*, which gave the surface a greater sheen, and eliminated differences in texture between one coloured area and another.

Dish depicting St George, after Donatello. Caffaggiolo, *c.* 1510 and (*opposite*) dish, Faenza, *c.* 1480.

Istoriato

The detailed pictorial style of decoration became known as *Istoriato* (narrative painting). As a style it was used widely in Italy, not only at Faenza and Castel Caffagiolo, but also at Deruta and Orvieto in Umbria, at Gubbio, Pesaro and Castel Durante in Urbino, and in Venice. Naturally each centre tended to produce wares with distinctive characteristics. Even so, there was a great deal of interchange between the centres, for not only were technical methods and motifs copied freely, but the craftsmen frequently moved from one workshop to another. However, experts can recognize the work of a number of master craftsmen on the basis of technique alone. Often border patterns give as good a clue as any to the place of origin. Sometimes the border was completely eliminated, the narrative painting being carried to the very edge of the dish. A limited number of plates bear the initials of the decorator on the reverse side, but few of them can be allocated to known artists. An even smaller number bear the full name of the decorator.

Deruta and Gubbio lustres

While the technical and artistic skills of narrative painting were being developed in the early sixteenth century, a limited number of potteries carried out experiments with lustre. These wares alone, strictly speaking, should be described as 'Maiolica', although the term is now more widely used to embrace all Italian tin-glazed wares of the Renaissance. The earliest Italian lustre wares appeared in Deruta shortly after 1500, as a direct imitation of the 'silver' lustres of Manises. The lustre was a brassy yellow and was normally used, again in imitation of Manises, with cobalt blue as the sole colour. By 1520 a far greater range of lustre colours was being produced in Gubbio, where they were introduced by Maestro Giorgio Andreoli, a native of Pavia. 'Gold', 'ruby' and 'silver' lustres were all used, and as at Deruta, normally with cobalt blue as the sole colour. At Gubbio, too, the iridescent effect of the lustre was occasionally heightened by modelling details in relief so that they caught the light, no matter from what angle it came. Apart from narrative painting, the workshops of Deruta and Gubbio produced a large number of dishes decorated with busts or profiles, most of which are clearly portraits.

Jug in lustreware. Deruta, c. 1520 and (*opposite*) dish with narrative decoration. Deruta, c. 1500.

Quese se fano a Vinegià et a Genona pinehe in un i stusghi
e pagotti il cento di lire

Nicola Pellipario

The work of Nicola Pellipario, a native of Castel Durante in Urbino, calls for particular consideration, for he evolved what was essentially a system of decoration that was to be copied during the following half century. Pellipario's early work, from about 1515, was of the rather sombre Faenza colouring, often showing that woodcuts were a source of subject matter. He already demonstrated a very considerable talent for painting landscapes as well as portraits. By 1528 he was working with his son, Guido Durantino, and radically changed his entire style of decoration. The sombre colours were rejected for warm oranges and yellows with shading in *grisaille*, essentially tones of cobalt blue, while relying heavily upon Raphael engravings for his compositions. Very similar in character were the products of Francesco Xanto Avelli da Rovigo, who 'lifted' figures from contemporary engravings, sometimes re-arranging them to suit his design, and who also was working in Urbino from 1530.

Cipriano Piccolpasso

Our understanding of the techniques used by Italian potters of this period has been helped enormously by a book written between 1555 and 1560 by Cipriano Piccolpasso, who prepared his treatise, *The Three Books of the Potter's Art*, for an influential patron, and happily the manuscript, complete with Piccolpasso's own line illustrations, is still in existence. The first book deals largely with clay and its preparation, and methods of shaping pottery using the wheel and moulds; the second book covers the preparation of glazes and colours, the construction of mills for grinding them, and the building of kilns; while the third book describes methods of painting and firing. At the end of the third book Piccolpasso illustrates the various styles of painting as commonly used in the different pottery centres of Italy, also giving the current prices then paid for such wares. Not only is the book an invaluable source of information about Italian tin-glazed wares, it is also very much a book of the Renaissance, comparable with the

(*above*) Dish by Pellipario, Castel Durante, 1532. (*below*) A page from *The Three Books of the Potter's Art* by Piccolpasso, *c*. 1560.

Dish by Lodovico.
Venice, c. 1545.

writings of Cellini and Vasari in the field of fine arts, in which
Piccolpasso derides the idea that processes of making pottery
can be kept a jealously guarded secret.

Pesaro and Lodovico

From the late fifteenth century Ming porcelain (see page 76)
began to be imported into Italy in small quantities. Copies in
tin glaze and decorated in deep cobalt blue, *alla porcellana*,
were made at a number of centres. As with the Chinese
originals, borders of leaves, peony and chrysanthemum flowers
were set around a scene of Chinese daily life. Probably under
the influence of imported Iznik (see page 81) and Persian
(see page 88) wares with coloured grounds, a very different
style of blue-and-white pottery was evolved in Venice in the
mid-sixteenth century. The tin glaze was itself tinted with
traces of cobalt and manganese to fire a pale lavender grey. On
this surface, decoration was carried out in deep cobalt blue
and in opaque white. Giacomo da Pesaro and Maestro Lodovico, both of whom commonly signed their work, were the
leading exponents of this type of decoration. A further innovation to be seen in these Venetian wares is in the use of
moulded rather than thrown forms. Many of the shapes
reflect those of metal tablewares of the period.

Bianchi di Faenza

Neither the narrative tradition of Urbino nor the blue-and-white of Venice were to have quite the impact on the rest of Europe as the type of pottery developed in Faenza in the late sixteenth century. These white wares, *bianchi di Faenza* or *faïence* as they became known, were frequently moulded, often with elaborate filigree patterns; or parts were moulded separately, as for example the spouts, handles and bases of jugs. Dishes, plates and jugs took on a far greater range of forms, with fluting and scalloped edges clearly derived from current metalwork. Furthermore, decoration was usually, but not invariably, reduced to a minimum. Thus, a dish might bear in its centre no more than a coat-of-arms, a spray of flowers or a hastily-sketched figure; the rim might be left bare or at most carry an unobtrusively repeat pattern. Motifs as a whole were largely derived from those of the Renaissance. All in all, the Faenza craftsmen removed pottery from the rôle of ornamenting walls and apothecaries' shelves and brought it back to the table where it belonged.

Dish in filigree work, Turin, *c.* 1580. Plate with floral decoration, Montelupo, *c.* 1600.

ISLAM UNDER THE OTTOMANS AND ITS INFLUENCE

Yüan and early Ming: celadons and porcelain

Exactly when the Chinese began to decorate porcelain in underglaze blue (cobalt) is uncertain: the earliest vessel known is dated 1351, and possibly blue-and-white porcelain may have been made as early as 1300. The pigment, known in China as 'Mohammedan blue', was imported from Persia either by way of the Great Silk Road (see page 43) or by sea through the south China ports. The wares, decorated with fish, birds, dragons or human figures, with sprays of leaves and flowers, were often embellished with touches of underglaze red (reduced copper). They were exported in great quantities, especially after the Mongols had been shaken off. Although Chinese blue-and-white porcelain was to have the greatest impact upon the pottery of the Middle East and Europe, T'zu-chou (see pages 42–45) and celadon (see pages 37–38) wares continued to be exported.

Blue-and-white Ming porcelain dish and celadon dish with unglazed reliefs and (*opposite*) bowl in the Mongol style from Sultānābād, all *c.* 1400.

Sultānābād and the 'Mongol Style' wares

The Mongol rulers of the Middle East brought with them their own style of ceramics, and from about 1300 onwards this can be seen in the hemispherical bowls made in the Sultānābād region. The vessels were covered with a dull brown or green-grey slip over which decoration was picked out in white slip, outlined in black, and covered with a clear glaze. Although animals were sometimes depicted, floral and geometric patterns were more common. The latter, which frequently included palmettes and arabesques, appear to have been inspired by designs used on textiles; the sombre colouring is reminiscent of the natural hairs of sheep and goats. In Persia, under Mongol domination, pottery continued to be made at Kashan in the late thirteenth century. The types of ware and the styles of decoration varied little from those current before the Mongol conquest (see pages 52 and 54). Designs carried out in underglaze painting in blue (cobalt), black and turquoise (copper) normally incorporated animals or human figures. The same motifs were used on lustre wares (see page 60), but their manufacture ceased by the end of the century.

'Damascus' and 'Miletus' wares

By the late fourteenth century a distinctive type of ware made of a white body and decorated in blue and black under a clear glaze was being produced in or near Damascus. These 'Damascus' wares included mosque lamps and drug-jars, usually decorated in horizontal zones. The potteries at Iznik (Nicea) were established rather earlier than those in Syria. How they came to be set up and by whom is obscure. In all probability the craftsmen were drawn from many places: Greeks, Armenians and Persians may all have contributed to the labour force. Initially the Iznik wares were made of a red body covered with a white slip. On this surface, decoration was carried out in blue (cobalt), black and green (copper) and covered with a clear glaze. This pottery, often referred to as 'Miletus' ware after the town in which it was first recognized, was thus technically identical to Persian and Byzantine under-glaze painted wares of earlier centuries (see pages 54 and 55). The style of decoration was, however, very different. Animals and human figures were not used at all; plant motifs and arabesques occur only very rarely, the normal decoration being of geometric patterns.

Early Iznik

In the two decades prior to 1500 the Iznik potters were evidently being influenced very considerably by the products of Damascus. The body used from now on was of white clay mixed with frit and a great deal of quartz. The underglaze colours were cobalt blue and black, the latter used for outlines; designs were limited to inscriptions, arabesques and plant motifs. Early Iznik and 'Damascus' pottery was doubtlessly influenced by Chinese blue-and-white porcelain, which must have been familiar to the Iznik potters, as it was to be found, by this time, throughout the Arab world, from Indonesia to Somaliland. Furthermore, the choice of flowers used for decoration, rather than a borrowing of complete motifs, would suggest the influence of Chinese porcelain. The Iznik potters, however, were far too dynamic to be content to be mere copyists: even if they were to reproduce the occasional design from Ming porcelain, that was to be all. They were soon to evolve their distinctive polychrome style with a bravura that was later to inspire many other potters.

(*opposite*) Earthenware jar with blue-and-white glaze, Damascus, *c.* 1500. (*below*) Iznik dish copying chinese porcelain, *c.* 1500.

Iznik: the 'Damascus' style

From about 1525 the Iznik potters began to increase the range of colours used in painting. At first manganese (purple) and iron pigments were employed, the latter firing from brown to sage green. To these were later added a variety of blues based upon cobalt and copper. Apart from dishes, the common shapes were spouted jugs, clearly derived from metallic forms; bowls with a low foot-ring, and others with a high cylindrical foot copying a Chinese form. To this period, too, belong a great number of hanging lamps from mosques, the latter normally decorated in zones of Cufic inscriptions and floral patterns. Domestic wares showed an ever-increasing concentration on floral designs incorporating grapes, tulips, carnations and the fritillary. Sprays of flowers are bunched to cover the whole decorated area, their stems emanating from a single point on the periphery of the design; veining on leaves and petals is often shown by scratching through the colour; while the points of tall, slender leaves are often doubled back to contain them within the circumference of the design. This superb, crisp style of floral painting reached its apogee in the middle of the sixteenth century, but it remains difficult to explain its inspiration.

Mosque lamp of Iznik ware dated to 1549.

Iznik: the 'Rhodian' style

By 1600 there were three hundred workshops at Iznik, and pottery had become very much a side-line to the manufacture of tiles, which were used in the building and restoring of mosques. The colours of the 'Damascus' style were difficult to control, and to meet the demands of mass-production a new palette was evolved in which black and cobalt blue were used with green based upon copper and red derived from a clay – Armenian bole, which at its best provides a brilliant sealing-wax red; when mismanaged it is a dirty brown covered with a bubbled glaze. Dishes were the major articles of production. Floral decoration, now almost invariably of the 'common root' type, was normally set against the white of the body, but coloured slips were also occasionally used as a background on which to carry out the floral design. Some five hundred dishes decorated in this style were bought for the Cluny Museum, France, in the nineteenth century from Lindos in Rhodes, where they had been the treasured possessions of many Greek households. It was thought, naturally, that they had been produced in the island, although this is now known not to be the case.

Jug and plate of Iznik ware in the Rhodian style, both c. 1600.

Late Iznik

In the early seventeenth century the frenzied building of mosques declined. By 1650 only nine workshops were still functioning at Iznik, and by 1724 the mere handful of craftsmen who remained were gathered up to man a tile factory in Istanbul. In the sixteenth century the Iznik potters had taken over the 'rock-and-wave' border of Chinese porcelain as a setting for floral patterns: a century later the border was still being used, now reduced to a meaningless scatter of spirals. Purely geometric motifs became common, while human figures, ships, and even buildings are found as central features of design, but even if the decline of Iznik is the story of a slow, painful death, at its height it had a profound influence upon European pottery. In the second half of the nineteenth century it was copied by Deck of Paris, by Minton in England, by Ulysse Cantagalli in Italy, and in Isfahan. It inspired William De Morgan (see page 146) and William Morris: and in our own century it has formed the basis of 'tourist' pottery. Chinese wares apart, no group of pottery has been so often copied, and so often faked, as that of Iznik at its prime.

Dish of late Iznik ware, c. 1650.

'Kubachi' wares: monochromes

Although the Persian wares of the 16th–17th century may be classified, exactly where each group was manufactured remains obscure. The earliest group of Persian pottery to be considered is the so-called 'Kubachi' ware. Kubachi is a small town in the Caucasus Mountains, once esteemed for the production of fine steel. Like the people of Lindos, the inhabitants of Kubachi had long treasured the decorated dishes which hung on the walls of their homes, later to sell them to dealers in the nineteenth century. In fact, the wares can never have been very satisfactory for they were made of an extremely soft white body covered with a heavily crackled glaze. The earliest of these dishes dated from perhaps the mid-fifteenth century and were decorated in underglaze black over which was applied a blue or green slip, a technique strongly resembling the slip-painted wares of thirteenth-century Rayy and Kashan (see page 52). By 1500, however, the 'Kubachi' potters were beginning to copy the heavy late Ming blue-and-white wares, detail by detail, although the copies usually show a softer, more rounded style than the Chinese prototypes.

Kubachi dish with black underglaze decoration, *c.* 1500.

'Kubachi' polychrome wares

Parallel with the development of 'Kubachi' blue-and-white was that of a polychrome style. The designs were drawn in black outline, blocked in with deep·cobalt blue, turquoise, deep manganese purple and ochre; and to this colour scheme was added, in about 1500, Armenian bole (see page 81). If the colouring was akin to that of Iznik, the same cannot be said of the subject-matter. The rims might be left plain or bear a 'Chinese' border pattern, but otherwise the trees, the figures and the flowers are an immediate borrowing from miniature painting. The production of 'Kubachi' wares ended, apparently abruptly, in about 1630. The historical reason is not known or where the pottery was manufactured. Tiles made of 'Kubachi' fabrics are known from north-west Persia, and although Tabriz is recorded as having been a centre of tile production, European travellers and traders of the late seventeenth century do not speak of Tabriz as a pottery centre, although others – Shiraz, Meshed, Yezd, Kirmān and Zarend – were sometimes mentioned, and it was the production of these cities that was to influence Europe.

'Kirmān' wares

Early in the sixteenth century the Portuguese held a trade concession with the south Persian port of Bender Abbas, a position usurped by the British in 1614. With the fall of the Ming dynasty in 1644, Dutch traders found it impossible to acquire Chinese porcelain, when they, too, began to trade in Persian wares through Bender Abbas. Naturally, since the demand was for Chinese porcelain, the more 'Chinese' the pottery, the better pleased were the dealers, and contemporary accounts make it quite clear that such pottery was being made in two cities, Kirmān and Meshed. Kirmān lies some 250 miles north of Bender Abbas and to the workshops of this city has been attributed a group of pottery with a body harder than that of 'Kubachi', covered with a slightly green glaze containing minute bubbles. The earliest known pottery of this type is dated 1523, though most of the pottery is clearly of the seventeenth century, copying late Ming landscape and still-life motifs in a deep cobalt blue. To these were often added purely 'Persian' details in red (Armenian bole), sage green (iron) and ochre – motifs again closely paralleled in Persian miniature paintings of the period.

Narghile of Kirmān ware of mixed Chinese and Persian styles, c. 1550 and (*opposite*) polychrome Kubachi dish, c. 1600.

'Meshed' wares

The second major group of Persian blue-and-white pottery approaches even more closely the Chinese originals than the 'Kirmān' wares. Made of a hard, pure white body, they are covered with a thin brilliant glaze. The designs are outlined with a fine black line filled in with shades of clear blue. The motifs, largely derived from late Ming wares, seem to lack any other source of inspiration; and there is no clearly detectable influence from Persian painting of the period, although some features, such as garments, have evidently been modified to be more intelligible to the decorators. Both the 'Kirman' and 'Meshed' wares commonly carry potters' marks in bogus Chinese characters. One type, the so-called 'tassel' mark, is derived from a single Chinese character, and usually takes the form of an elaborate squiggle with a long tail, normally painted in blue. The other common mark copies the Chinese reign-mark of six characters contained within a square cartouche, normally so poorly executed that it is impossible to tell which reign-mark was meant. Clearly the intention was to allow the wares to be passed off as 'genuine Chinese'.

Bowl of Meshed ware closely copying Chinese porcelain, *c.* 1600.

Spouted cup of Persian lustreware, *c.* 1800.

Late Persian lustre wares

As a class of pottery the Persian lustre wares are quite distinct
from all other seventeenth-century Persian pottery and owe
nothing to Chinese influence. The vessels were made of a com-
pact white body covered with a glaze slightly tinged green.
The lustre patterns were laid down either on the white glazed
surface or on one of a deep, warm blue. Often bowls, for
example, would be glazed white on the inside and blue on the
outer surface. Common motifs included the iris, willow and
cypress trees, peacocks and animals, especially deer. The
vessels were mostly small, perhaps to fit the dimensions of the
muffle kiln in which they were lustred, and included many
shapes not to be found in the blue-and-white wares: coffee
cups, egg-cups and tall, slender-necked bottles for wine.
Where in Persia they were made is unknown, but the presence
of so many wine bottles in this ware suggests Shiraz, the
birthplace of Omar Khayyām, and a region where there were
many vineyards.

Persian wares with coloured grounds

In seventeenth-century Persia some copies of celadons were made that, at a distance, could pass for the real thing. Coloured grounds – rich blue, turquoise, emerald and golden brown – were used, sometimes left plain and sometimes decorated with floral motifs in opaque white. One group of these wares, with a rich blue ground decorated with white carnations and touches of yellow ochre, made from the mid to late seventeenth century, were to be copied by Hungarian (see page 102) and French (see page 104) potters working in tin glaze. The idea of using deep blue grounds may have derived ultimately from a group of Chinese imports. These were late Ming porcelain wares against the blue background of which were set floral designs in coloured glazes, each colour contained within incised lines. More directly inspired by these brightly coloured Chinese vessels, however, is a group of seventeenth-century Persian pottery that could best be described as confectionery; mostly bottles of fantastic shapes and small spouted jugs.

Narghile (*left*) with coloured ground, and scent bottle (*right*) with coloured glazes and moulded decoration, both *c.* 1800.

Canak Kale and Kutahya

Records show that Armenian potters in the small township of Kutahya, seventy-five miles south-east of Iznik, were already at work by 1608. Their production was always partly devoted to making tiles, but cups, bottles and decorated dishes were also produced. Technically the Kutahya wares are identical to those of Iznik, being of the same brilliant white body decorated with the 'Rhodian' palette (see page 81). The style of decoration, however, was quite different. Apart from the use of figures drawn in a child-like manner, the common system of decoration was one using a repeat pattern of floral sprays. By the nineteenth century, the Kutahya workshops were making bad copies of European porcelain. At the same time a second Turkish pottery, Canak Kale on the Bosporus, also began to produce 'peasant porcelain' in red earthenware covered with a white slip. In 1920 a group of Kutahya potters moved to Jerusalem, ostensibly to make tiles for the restoration of the Dome of the Rock Mosque. Instead it was found more profitable to make 'Iznik' wares for tourists (see page 82).

Water-bottle from Canak Kale, Turkey, c. 1800.

Mug with pewter lid (*left*) and dish (*right*) of Haban ware, dated 1618 and 1615.

EUROPEAN FAIENCE: THE ITALIAN ABROAD
Haban: Faenza style

By the mid-sixteenth century Italian potters, largely *Nuovi Cristiani*, as well as others of Swabian origin, set up workshops in western Hungary to produce faïence wares. Generally known as the Haban, a name derived from the Hebrew, meaning 'Children of God', the potters were members of a 'Brotherhood' whose Anabaptist creed dictated what they might produce in the way of decoration. Human and animal figures were forbidden and only the simplest of floral decoration or coats-of-arms were permitted. By the early seventeenth century Haban workshops were to be found not only scattered throughout western Hungary, but also at Alvinc in Transylvania. Initially their wares showed strong Italian influence: dishes with flutings or open filigree work were moulded (see page 75) and decorated in underglaze colours with patterns clearly derived from Renaissance Italy, or with the armorial bearings of their patrons, but from about 1620 onwards the use of floral patterns became increasingly common.

Haban: floral style

For the greater part of the seventeenth century the Haban potters produced faïence decorated in a floral style that was both distinctive and precocious. The insistence on simplicity of decoration ensured that large areas of their wares were left in undecorated white tin glaze with a few sprays of flowers which were often contained within bands of cobalt blue. Apart from tulips and carnations borrowed from Iznik sources (see page 80), the motifs were clearly copied directly from contemporary engravings. The designs were drawn in very fine black lines, and blocked in with blue (cobalt), green (copper), amber (ochre) and yellow (antimony), the final result often having the appearance of a pen-and-wash watercolour sketch. The usual Haban shapes were plates and dishes, square and hexagonal jars, jugs with ovoid bodies, and tall beer mugs with slightly concave profiles. The jugs were often provided with pewter lids, the products also of Haban craftsmen. The study of Haban pottery is greatly simplified by the fact that the great majority of vessels bear the date of manufacture, the initial figure '1' frequently being replaced by the Gothic letter 'H' – the monogram of 'Haban'.

Plate (*left*) and mug with pewter lid (*right*), dated 1616 and 1640.

Nuremberg

In the earlier part of the sixteenth century, at Nuremberg and elsewhere, lead-tin-glazed tiles were being made for stoves, and by 1525 a limited amount of tableware was being produced. Despite the fact that the technique was clearly inspired by the Urbino school (see page 72) with its predominant use of blue *grisaille* and ochres, the subject-matter was largely copied from woodcuts and engravings.

Winterthur

Shortly before the end of the sixteenth century, faïence tablewares began to be made at Winterthur in Switzerland. The favoured motifs, such as scrolls, plants and fruit, as well as the colouring, are typical of the Urbino school.

Lyons

Italian potters are known to have been established in Lyons as early as 1512, although nothing is known of their work. Even towards the end of the sixteenth century Italians were still emigrating to Lyons, so that its potteries did not develop any very distinctive features of their own. Admittedly, subjects for *Istoriato* painting were taken from local sources, such as the engravings of Soloman Bernard, but in style and technique Lyons remained very much an offshoot of Urbino. By 1575, *bianchi di faenza* was also being made at Lyons.

Nîmes

Although the Huguenot potter, Antoine Sigalon, who worked at Nîmes between 1548 and 1590, was a Frenchman, the products of his workshop – decorated in sombre deep blue, orange and ochre – are barely distinguishable from those of Faenza. The main output of his pottery was of dishes and drug-jars decorated with coats-of-arms. During the same period a workshop owned by Pierre Estève of Montpellier, which had a thriving medical school, was also producing drug-jars of a very similar character.

Drug-jar of Nîmes faïence, Sigalon's factory, *c.* 1550 and (*opposite*) dish of Lyons faïence, 1582.

Rouen

A second potter making faïence in France was Masseot Abaquesne of Rouen, who worked between 1530 and 1560. Although his main concern was the production of tiles, records show that in 1545 he supplied an apothecary in Rouen with five thousand drug-jars; very few vessels of this type have survived. They are decorated in the Urbino style, usually with profile heads painted in pale blues and yellows.

Both Sigalon and Abaquesne must have learnt their craft in Italy or from emigrant Italians. Curiously, however, neither workshop continued long after their owners' deaths. When faïence began again to be made in Rouen it was entirely changed.

Nevers

In about 1585 a family of Genoese potters, the Conrades of Albissola, began work at Nevers, and in 1603 they obtained a thirty-year monopoly. During this period the Conrades produced *Istoriato* decorated wares, similar to those of Lyons (see page 92). When the monopoly expired, other factories were set up, and the newcomers brought with them novel ideas of design, amongst which were features of the Italian Baroque. Jars and jugs were provided with moulded spouts and handles in the form of grotesque masks and beasts, all clearly derived from contemporary silverware, as too were many of the shapes. From about 1640 onwards, jars of late Ming shape were being made, often decorated with *Istoriato* subjects. Nevers faïence is, above all, unusual for the quality of its colouring which relied upon soft blues, orange and yellow with a little green. No red was used, but outlines and shading were done in purple (manganese). Even when copying Chinese blue-and-white, outlines were drawn in purple,

Faïence jar copying a Chinese shape, Nevers, *c.* 1650. (*opposite*) Dish by Cornelius Lubbertszoon of Haarlem, dated 1583.

a technique also used at Delft (see page 96). Yet a third influence was soon to be felt, for from about 1650 Persian styles were to dominate the products of Nevers (see page 104).

Netherlandish faïence: Antwerp and Haarlem

The establishment of faïence workshops in Antwerp was largely due to the Italian families, Andries(z) and Floris. In 1512 Guido Andriesz of Casteldurante set up a factory largely for the production of tiles, but it also made useful wares such as drug-jars in the deep blue, green, orange and yellow colours, so typical of Faenza. In 1564 one son of Andriesz founded a workshop at Middelburg in Holland, and another son a factory at Lambeth in England in 1571 (see page 99). A second factory in Holland was established at Haarlem in 1573, where again the products were essentially Italian in feeling and technique. The rival Floris workshop concentrated rather on a decorative style based on strapwork derived from the local school of engravers. It appears that the potteries in Antwerp failed to survive the Sack of 1576, and it was from Haarlem that the impetus for further development of faïence in the Low Countries was to come.

Delft: the Oriental School

Imports of Chinese porcelain through the Dutch East India Company resulted in a large part of the early output of Delft potters being copies or imitations of Chinese wares. As at Nevers, blue-and-white wares were first outlined in purple or black (*trek*). Often, too, the wares received a second glazing similar to *coperta* (see page 69) and known as *kwaart*. The backs of plates and dishes, which had initially been covered only with a clear lead glaze, were now covered in lead-tin white. Although at first the Haarlem potters were content to incorporate decorative features of imported Chinese wares into what was otherwise an essentially Netherlandish pattern, by the middle of the seventeenth century remarkably accurate copies of Chinese wares were being made. For a century patterns of Chinese origin remained the predominant choice of the Delft potters, but from 1641 they turned also to copying Kakiemon and Imari porcelains. Due to a decline in the brewing trade in Delft, the old breweries had gradually been taken over as potteries, usually retaining their original names – 'Stag', 'Rose', 'Three Bells', and so on. These names, or their symbols, were commonly used as potters' marks.

Delft polychrome dish copying Chinese polychrome porcelain.

Delft: the Dutch School

Side by side with copies of Oriental porcelain the Delft potters evolved their own particularly 'Dutch' style of decoration. Their palette was largely blue-and-white, while the subject matter was frequently lifted directly from the engravings after Raphael or by artists of the Dutch School. Paintings were copied, too, especially those of Berghem, Mommers, Rembrandt and Van Ruysdael. Landscapes and religious subjects were very common, but even scenes depicting various industries such as the tobacco trade were occasionally used. Amongst the earliest wares painted in this style in the 1660s were those of Frederick van Frijtom (Frytom) whose rather crowded landscapes were original compositions. A decade later Arendt Cosijn produced a number of finely decorated wares which relied heavily upon engravings for their subject matter. The same reliance on engravings is seen in the work of Dochus Hoppestein of the 'Moor's Head', at the end of the century. This style of decoration was, of course, the inspiration for the tile industry.

Delft plate copying a design by Goltzius, c. 1690.

'Malling', Aldgate and Southwark

The first potters to produce faïence in England were probably of Flemish origin, and their work is only known by a small number of jugs with speckled tin glaze made in imitation of imported Rhenish stonewares (see page 111). Their silver or pewter lids and mounts show them to have been made from the 1550s onwards. Because an example of this type of jug came from West Malling church, they are known generically as 'Malling' wares, although their place of manufacture is quite unknown. Their manufacture probably ceased during the reign of Mary Tudor. In 1567 two Flemish potters, Jacob Janson (Jansz) and Jaspar Andries (see page 95) set up a pottery in Norwich about which nothing is known, although it was still in operation a century later. A number of small jugs in blue and ochre floral designs, copying Chinese blue-and-white imports, and rather squat drug-jars decorated in simple blue and ochre patterns, many coming from London Wall, may be from the Aldgate workshops. In 1625 Christian Wilhelm set up a pottery in Southwark. This workshop was responsible for a group of wares similar in style to the earlier Delft imitations of late Ming porcelain (see page 96).

Malling jar (left), c. 1550, and faïence dish, perhaps by Janson, dated 1600. (*opposite*) Wine bottle, dated 1652, and drug-jar, c. 1720, both probably from Lambeth.

Early English delftware

In 1650 two Southwark potters established a workshop at Brislington, near Bristol, and in about 1665 the production of 'delftware' began at Lambeth, presumably by immigrant potters from Delft. In 1683 Edward Ward of Brislington set up the Temple pottery at Bristol, and two years later the Burlington pottery was founded in New Jersey, U.S.A., presumably by other craftsmen from Brislington. By 1700 two further workshops were established in Bristol. In view of the short intervals between the foundation of these potteries, it is hardly surprising that it is very difficult to distinguish between the wares made in these centres, but the distinction between Delft and English 'delft' is more easily made. By comparison the English wares are clumsy and often inept, although the range of motifs – sketchy flower decorations and landscapes, derived from Delft, or direct copies of Chinese blue-and-white and *famille verte* porcelain – closely followed those of Delft itself. English delftware of this period has a rustic charm, but lacks the sophistication of the Dutch.

Blue dash dish, Lambeth, *c.* 1670.

'Blue dash' dishes

Between the mid-seventeenth and opening decade of the eighteenth centuries Lambeth and Bristol potters made large decorative dishes, often quaintly called 'blue dash chargers'. The term 'blue dash' derives from the habit of decorating the rim with a series of oblique strokes of blue. This motif comes ultimately from Chinese porcelain, although it is to be found on Italian, French and Delft faïence. The dishes were provided with a flat foot rim, which was commonly either bored or given a groove around its circumference for suspension. Many of the dishes bear portraits of the English kings and queens from Charles I to Queen Anne, often only recognizable by the royal insignia. More remarkable than these, however, are large dishes painted in floral designs in blue, green, ochre and purple, which, unlike the portrait dishes, seem to owe nothing to contemporary wares in Western Europe. The flowers depicted are normally tulips and carnations. Although typically insular in execution, these dishes were clearly inspired by Iznik models.

Hanau and Frankfurt

In Germany the development of faïence during the seventeenth century was inspired by a number of alien sources. As the Hanse-town of Hamburg carried much of the trade between Portugal and northern Europe, a large part of the Hamburg pottery evidently copied the blue-and-white faïence made in Lisbon or relied upon its wares for decorative motifs. From the middle of the century, however, the influence of Delft began to be felt. In 1661 immigrant Dutch craftsmen set up a pottery in Hanau, and five years later a workshop was opened in Frankfurt by a Parisian, Jean Simonet. The latter pottery was very soon taken over by a German, Johann Fehr, under whose guidance excellent blue-and-white wares in the Chinese idiom, and using a *coperta* (*kwaart*) overglaze, surpassed in quality even those of Delft. Until the early years of the eighteenth century a part of the decoration of the Hanau and Frankfurt pottery was undertaken by outside decorators, the *Hausmaler*. Their original training had been in the 'painting' of window-glass for which Nuremberg was renowned. Decoration in this technique was also applied to stonewares (see page 114). By the 1680s there were two faïence workshops in Berlin both copying the Delft styles.

Blue-and-white faïence dishes from Hanau (*left*) and Frankfurt (*right*), both c. 1680.

EUROPEAN FAIENCE: THE EIGHTEENTH CENTURY
Haban ware

From the mid-seventeenth century onwards the Haban potters of Alvinc (see page 90) found themselves increasingly influenced by late Iznik and Persian decoration. At times this amounted to little more than using a coloured lead-tin ground – yellow, lavender blue or deep blue, on which were painted their normal floral motifs (see page 91). More typically Persian, however, was a decoration carried out in opaque white on a dark blue ground, in which zones of a fish-scale pattern were sometimes included. When the Turks overran Hungary in 1663, many of the Haban potters were dispersed, some finding their way to Delft. With help from sympathizers in Holland and the Palatinate some potteries were re-established in the following decade. Their arrival coincided with a general relaxation of the rules of the 'Brotherhood', and with the final expulsion of the Turks in 1686, the distinctive features of Haban pottery became submerged beneath a welter of decoration, now including animals and human figures.

Jug (*left*) and plate (*right*) of Haban ware, dated 1674 and 1696. (*opposite*) Plate from Rouen in the *style rayonnant, c.* 1700.

Rouen and the *style rayonnant*

In 1647 Edmé Poterat obtained a monopoly for the production of faïence in Normandy and opened a workshop in Rouen. Of his early products nothing is known, but by the last quarter of the seventeenth century he had hit upon a system of decoration in blue-and-white that appeared sophisticated yet required little skill for its production. This *style rayonnant* was based upon lozenges of solid colour with jagged or scalloped outline (lambrequins) or pendants radiating from the edge towards the centre of a plate or dish, alternate motifs often being in blue-on-white and white-on-blue. The design was sometimes embellished with details in a rather gummy-looking red. With the Edict ordering the melting of all gold and silver in 1709, the Rouen potters found themselves producing greater quantities of these wares to replace not only plates and dishes, but also salt-cellars, dredgers, cisterns and soap trays. In all probability demand was such that there was a genuine shortage of skilled decorators, but by using the same motif – the lambrequin – repeatedly, this lack was overcome.

Nevers and *bleu persan*

The Iznik (see page 81) and Persian (see page 88) potters frequently used coloured tin glaze as a ground on which to paint; the same technique had been adopted by Italian (see page 74) and Haban (see page 102) potters. In about 1670 the technique was taken up by some potteries at Nevers (see page 94). Usually a deep blue (*bleu persan*) was employed, over which details were painted in opaque white, yellow and orange. The motifs most commonly found are floral sprays and birds, copied – often with considerable alterations – from Chinese blue-and-white porcelain. The technique proved a rather difficult one to master, probably because the opaque colours applied as decoration had to be laid down quite thickly, with the result that on objects, other than plates and dishes which could be fired flat, there was a tendency for the glaze to 'weep' causing the decoration to slip downwards. Nevertheless, the *bleu persan* of Nevers enjoyed a considerable vogue. It was copied extensively at Rouen and by the Delft potteries as well as in England. Although Nevers is remembered during this period for its *bleu persan*, a large part of its production was devoted to blue-and-white designs reflecting current tastes.

Jug from Nevers in the *bleu persan* style, *c*. 1680.

(*opposite*) Plate from the Clérissy factory, Moustiers, in the *style Bérain*, *c*. 1710.

Moustiers and the *style Bérain*

In 1679 Pierre Clérissy set up a workshop at Moustiers, a village in the foothills of the Alpes Maritimes, some one hundred kilometres north-east of Marseilles. Why he chose this remote location remains something of a mystery. For the first thirty years the Moustiers workshop produced fine, but unremarkable, blue-and-white wares, usually pictorial. The subject-matter was normally copied directly from contemporary engravings, as for example, the *Labours of Hercules* of Frans Floris, Leclerc's illustrations for the Bible, or Antonio Tempesta's hunting scenes. In about 1710, however, the potteries at Moustiers began to adapt the engravings of Jean Bérain, Designer to the King. The framework was often a pastiche incorporating busts, masks, grotesques and cherubs; birds and small animals; urns, pillars and arches; draped cloth and spindles. Decoration in the *style Bérain* had, like the *style rayonnant* and *bleu persan*, an enormous vogue, lasting until the 1740s, during which period it was copied widely, even as far afield as in Spain and Italy.

Dish from Alcora, Spain, *c.* 1720.

Moustiers and Alcora

Throughout the seventeenth century Spanish potters assimilated some of the trends current in European faïence, but nowhere more successfully than at Talavera de la Reina in Toledo. These wares were carried out in polychrome, the subject matter being borrowed from the engravings of Johannes Stradanus and, later, Antonio Tempesta. Hunting scenes and bull-fights were particularly popular, the picture often covering the entire decorated surface. In 1727 the Count of Aranda set up a new workshop at Alcora, north of Paterna, relying partly upon craftsmen attracted from Talavera and partly upon master-potters from France: Edward Roux from Moustiers and Joseph Olerys from Marseilles. Olerys introduced the current *style Bérain* to the Alcora potters; twelve years later he returned to France, this time to Moustiers, bringing with him the knowledge of Talavera and Alcora polychrome painting. It is difficult to distinguish at a glance between the products of Alcora and those made at Moustiers after 1739, although the body of the former is red as opposed to the buff body of the latter.

Strasbourg and the *fleurs des Indes*

In 1721 Charles-François Hannong set up a faïence workshop at Strasbourg. The early products of this pottery were not remarkable, often being no more than rather poorly executed blue-and-white wares in the *style rayonnant*. His son, Paul-Antoine, took over direction in 1739 introducing a few other colours such as yellow, green and red, and in 1744 gilding was used sparingly. The year 1748 was a turning-point in the history of European faïence, for in that year discontented decorators from the Meissen porcelain factory (see page 115) joined Hannong's staff at Strasbourg, bringing with them the secrets of painting in overglaze 'enamels'. This system was largely used for flower decoration. The simpler to execute, and thus the more common, were the *fleurs des Indes* – stylized flowers based upon Chinese porcelain-painting. Outlines and shading were carried out in black with the polychrome colours laid on in graded washes. By contrast the *fleurs fines*, taken largely from botanical works of the period, had neither outlines nor shading in black.

Plate decorated with *fleurs des Indes*, Strasbourg, *c.* 1770.

Late English delftware

A pottery making delftware was established at Liverpool in 1710: by the mid-century there were a dozen in the city. Other factories included those at Wincanton (1730), Dublin (1737), Glasgow (1748) and Limerick (1762). Designers, while still following the fashions at Delft, looked more and more to France for inspiration. Thus from about 1740 there was a short vogue for *bleu persan* decoration and at much the same time decorators began to use the softer colours of French Rococo pottery. A decade later, the Swede, Magnus Lundberg, introduced the technique of *bianco-sopra-bianco* in which the opaque white design was normally laid down on a ground tinted pale blue or lavender grey. First used at Lambeth, it was copied after 1755 in Bristol. For a brief period, shortly before 1760, a brighter palette comprising French blue, violet, olive-green, lemon and clear red, was used for floral decorations. Liable to chip and easily scratched, delftware could not, however, hold its own against white stonewares (see page 118), which were more serviceable, and creamwares (see page 129), which were cheaper.

Plate with *bianco-sopra-bianco* border, Bristol, *c.* 1750.

Jar with cover, Fulda,
Germany, *c*. 1770.

Sceaux and Fulda: the end of faïence

Due to bad management, production at Strasbourg ceased in
1754, but the tradition of flower painting was continued in
many faïence workshops, most notably that of Veuve Perrin
at Marseilles and at Niderviller, founded by the Baron de
Beyerlé in 1748. The workshops at Fulda, founded in 1741,
and at Höchst, established five years later, produced some
outstanding work. In Scandinavia the potteries at Copenhagen
and at Rörstrand, Sweden, set up in 1721 and 1726 respec-
tively, were by the mid-century closely copying French and
German styles, although transfer-printing was introduced at
Rörstrand in 1767, only a few years after its development in
England (see page 131). The impact of imported English
creamwares, however, was too great to allow faïence production to be sustained, and by 1780 the potters at Delft had
already begun to copy these wares. Even as late as 1830, van
Putten and Co., an amalgamation of three once-prosperous
workshops, was still producing faïence. This, however, was a
swan-song, and for most European workshops in the 1780s
the choice was simply one of changing over to creamware
production, or of becoming insolvent.

EUROPEAN STONEWARES
Frankfurt and Cologne

In Europe the development of stonewares depended largely upon deposits of very plastic refractory clays found in the Westerwald and in the Rhine Valley, between Frankfurt and Cologne. These clays had been used by medieval potters from the ninth century, but were fired only to the low temperatures required of earthenware. It was discovered, however, that by firing to a higher temperature, a hard impervious body could be produced that needed no glaze to make it watertight, and which would not melt in the kiln. From the twelfth century onwards considerable quantities of cooking-pots, jugs and mugs were being made of this ware in the Rhineland. Typical forms were rather squat little jugs and mugs with rounded bodies covered with a mass of horizontal grooves and with a broad foot moulded like the edge of a pie-crust. By the end of the fourteenth century potters began throwing salt into the kiln fire when it reached its highest temperature. The salt volatilized and formed a thin film of alkaline glaze over the surface of their wares and by repeated additions of salt the glaze could be made thicker.

Stoneware jug, or *Jakobakanne*, probably Siegburg, *c.* 1500.

(*opposite*) Detail from Brueghel's *Peasant Wedding* showing typical stoneware jugs of the period *c.* 1570.

'Cologne' salt glaze

From the fifteenth century onwards, stonewares in the Rhineland were not only used locally but also became a considerable article of trade. The chief centres of production were at Höhr and Grenzhausen in the Westerwald; at Siegburg and Frechen near Cologne; and at Raeren near Aachen. The wares made in these towns were typically Gothic in feeling, generally being rather dumpy little vessels, although a taller and more elegant form of jug, the *Jakobakanne*, began to be made from about 1400 onwards. Even so, the vessels often illustrated by Pieter Brueghel (1525–1569) in his paintings of peasant life must be seen as the more usual output of the Rhenish potters. The makers of stoneware were, however, being influenced increasingly by two other local industries, those of bronze founding and the making of pewter, and wares which had initially been plain now began to be embellished with impressed designs. At times the designs were taken directly from coins, medals or seals impressed into the damp body, or stamps reminiscent of those used for butter were used.

Siegburg: white stonewares

In the early part of the six-teenth century, features of Renaissance design began to be felt in the Rhineland, and the effect, particularly of gold- and silversmiths, can be seen in vessels such as the so-called *bellarmine* (*Bart-mannkrug*) decorated with a heavily bearded face below the neck, and the moulded, long-spouted jug (*Schnabel-kanne*), ornately decorated in relief. The tall, slender, slight-ly tapering tankard (*Schnelle*) is probably derivative of local wooden vessels, although the relief decoration often shows features that were clearly drawn from Renaissance art. A second source of decorative subject-matter were the en-gravings of the Nuremberg school of artists, some of whom actually provided mod-els for the potters to copy, shaping naturally being done by the use of moulds. While the natural clays of Cologne and Frechen fired grey, and those of Raeren to a dark brown, at Siegburg a deposit of suitable clay was found which fired almost pure white. With the import of white wares from China and Italy it was only to be expected that the Siegberg potters should have exploited this clay deposit.

Raeren: underglaze colours

The first recorded use of underglaze colours on European stoneware was by Jan Emens Mennicken of Raeren, who in 1587 used a limited amount of cobalt blue as a backgrounding to low relief decoration confined with horizontal zones or oval or circular motifs. At a slightly later date manganese purple was used, and from the end of the sixteenth century other Rhenish potters used cobalt and manganese separately or together, these being the only two colours that could withstand the high temperatures of salt-glazing. The workshops at Raeren were responsible for a whole range of jugs with cylindrical bodies, narrow necks and sub-conical bases decorated with friezes or zones of religious or allegorical scenes, in which the figures were picked out in blue or purple. The manufacture of salt-glazed stonewares was to suffer a severe set-back during the Thirty Years' War: Siegburg and Raeren were devastated in the 1930s and a number of potters moved to Höhr and Grenzhausen in the Westerwald. The underglaze coloured stonewares remained, nevertheless, only a small part of their production. More typical was the *bellarmine*, a simple ovoid body with a narrow tapering neck on which was impressed a greatly simplified bearded mask.

(*opposite*) Moulded tankard (*Schnelle*) and jug (*Schnabelkanne*) in white stoneware. Siegburg, dated 1559 and 1590.

Stoneware drug-jar with underglaze blue decoration. Raeren, dated 1591.

Kreussen: 'enamelled' stonewares

In 1512 a family of Austrian potters, the Vests, moved to Kreussen in Franconia to begin the manufacture of stonewares. Their early work is unremarkable but in the early seventeenth century the Kreussen potters began to use the overglaze 'enamels' developed by the Nuremberg glassworkers (see page 101). These colours – blue, red, yellow, white and green – were highly fusible glasses applied as frits in a second firing to the previously salt-glazed wares. The most common form on which these colours were used were rather squat tankards, surfaced with a dark brown or black slip, to which pewter lids were normally attached. These were decorated with friezes of applied relief figures coloured with touches of 'enamel'. Contemporary with the Kreussen 'enamelled' stonewares were those made at Freiberg and other centres in Saxony, where the grey stoneware was frequently used without a covering slip under the glaze, while the 'enamel' colours were restricted to black and white. Wares of this genre are still produced today.

Enamelled stoneware jug with moulded decoration. Kreussen, c. 1650.

Böttger: red stoneware

In the closing years of the seventeenth century two of the most extraordinary characters in the history of ceramics were to concern themselves with the manufacture of stonewares – John Dwight and Johann Friedrich Böttger. As a young man, Böttger (b. 1682) worked for an apothecary in Berlin where, as a self-styled alchemist, he claimed to be able to transmute the baser metals into gold. Escaping from the clutches of William of Prussia, he was imprisoned by Augustus of Saxony. His experiments having failed, in 1704 he began work on the synthesis of precious stones, and three years later produced nothing more dramatic than red stoneware. Nevertheless, so convinced was he of its high value that the wares were cut and polished by lapidaries. The body was, in fact, a mixture of refractory and red clays similar to those used in Delft, but when, in 1708, he replaced the red clay with a white one (kaolin) from Meissen, he had hit upon the secret of porcelain. Augustus the Strong was quick to capitalize upon the discovery, setting up the Meissen factory in 1710.

Red stoneware bottle made by Böttger, Meissen, c. 1710.

Dwight of Fulham

John Dwight (b. 1637), like Böttger, had no training as a potter. He was, however, a shrewd businessman and in 1671, the same year in which an embargo was placed upon the importation of stonewares into Britain, he took out a patent on the manufacture of stoneware and set up a workshop in Fulham. Presumably relying upon imported Dutch labour, the main production was of red and grey stonewares technically similar to those of Holland and the Rhine. Dwight's avowed aim, however, was to produce porcelain, or as close an imitation as he could manage, and he set to work on experiments designed to provide a truly white stoneware body. His notebooks show that in the 1690s he was using sifted, calcined flint in place of white sand mixed with his clay, since this material gave a whiter body, a practice not to be introduced until 1720 in Staffordshire. Although his patent was renewed in 1684, Dwight was not alone in making stonewares in England, and in 1693 he brought a lawsuit against the Elers Brothers of Fulham (see page 117), the three Wedgwood Brothers of Burslem and James Morley of Nottingham for infringement of his monopoly.

The Elers Brothers and James Morley

John Philip and David Elers came to England in about 1688 and presumably set about making stoneware at Fulham forthwith. Following Dwight's lawsuit of 1693 they removed to Bradwell Wood in Staffordshire where suitable clays were to be had and their activities would be less conspicuous. Here, in an atmosphere of almost demented secrecy, they set about producing dry red stonewares and brown salt-glazed wares, paying great attention to the washing and mixing of clays to provide a body of fine grain size, a practice not then known in Staffordshire. Their wares, like those of Holland, were turned on a lathe when green-hard and decorated with sprigs made in moulds of brass or alabaster. The term 'Elers Ware' has come to be used to describe not only their products but those of later imitators. Less is known about James Morley, a co-defendant in the Dwight suit. Nottingham had long been renowned for its pottery (see page 58), and an advertisement of about 1700 shows that Morley was selling cups, teapots and mugs decorated with incised flower-patterns. Surviving pottery of the period shows that this was a fine stoneware, covered with a red slip and salt-glazed. Production ceased in about 1800.

White saltglaze mug (*bottom*) by Dwight, about 1670; red stoneware mug (*centre*), perhaps by Elers, about 1695; and red stoneware coffee-pot (*top*), Staffordshire, *c*. 1730.

John and Thomas Astbury: white salt-glazed stonewares

John Astbury (1686–1743) was reputedly at one time employed by the Elers Brothers. During this time he is said to have assumed such an air of indifference to the whole business that he managed to gain complete access to the Elers' secrets of manufacture. In 1710 John Philip Elers left Staffordshire, and Astbury established his own pottery at Shelton where he made both lead-glazed earthenwares (see page 128) and stonewares. Whatever the truth of the tale about the Elers and Astbury, there is little doubt that the Elers left behind them an important legacy: sprig moulds, salt-glazing and, most vital of all, the knowledge that clays required to be refined before high quality wares could be made from them. Local Staffordshire clays and sands could produce, however, only drab buff wares, the so-called 'crouch' wares. To John Astbury and his son Thomas are attributed the introduction of ground calcined flint and white Devonshire clay into the body to provide a truly white ware, which first appeared in any quantity in the 1730s. Both these materials are said to have been discovered as the result of their use when dosing horses.

Stoneware plate and teapot,
Staffordshire, *c.* 1730.

Enamelled white plate and teapot. Staffordshire, c. 1760.

English 'enamelled' white stonewares

Plaster of Paris moulds, said to have been introduced into Staffordshire in 1750, had an enormous advantage since the stoneware body could be poured into the assembled mould as a slip. Until 1750 salt-glazed wares had been decorated entirely in relief, but from then on colour decoration was to gain increasing importance. For a brief period simple floral patterns were scratched into the body and the lines filled with powdered cobalt pigments before firing and glazing. The use of overglaze 'enamels', however, was on its way. Traditionally first introduced by two Dutchmen in about 1740, by 1760 English porcelain workshops were providing most of the 'enamellers'. At its best Staffordshire salt-glazed white stoneware has never been surpassed, and in its day it enjoyed a considerable vogue in Europe, where its superior quality to that of faïence was quickly appreciated. It contained, however, the seeds of its own undoing, for the body from which it was made was to provide a more economic ware (see page 132). In 1750 more than fifty Staffordshire potteries were making it: by 1780 it had all but gone out of production

EUROPEAN EARTHENWARE: THE MEDIEVAL HANGOVER
Sgraffiato wares of Renaissance Italy

Exactly when the *sgraffiato* wares of Islam and Byzantium began to be copied in Italy is obscure, but in Northern Italy their production probably began in the thirteenth century (see page 55). By the fifteenth century the technique of decoration was widespread, and the remains of workshops have been found, for example, at Padua and near Verona. Early examples show a technique identical to that of Byzantium or Syria in which the *sgraffiato* design was emphasized with areas of ochre or copper green. Motifs were typically Gothic, with heavy foliage, heraldic beasts and coats-of-arms predominating. During the sixteenth century, although influenced by Renaissance tin-glazed wares, the makers of *sgraffiato* pottery seldom attempted to copy them closely. The potters of Bologna seem to have been exceptional in that human figures and even caricature portraits were used with elaborate borders directly imitating current tin-glazed wares.

Sgraffiato dish with the arms of Narni, Umbrian. *c.* 1540.
(*opposite*) *Sgraffiato* dish made in north Devonshire. *c.* 1750.

Sgraffiato wares in Europe

The *sgraffiato* technique was in widespread use in the late Middle Ages in Europe as a means of decorating tiles, and the method was probably adopted by many potters as a way of ornamenting their wares quite independently of its development in Italy. By the end of the seventeenth century *sgraffiato* wares were being made in many widely dispersed centres – at Beauvais, at Krefeld in the Rhineland, at Langnau in Switzerland, and in north Devonshire. The latter potteries provided wares for some of the English colonies in North America, and an example excavated at Jamestown bears a floral decoration that stems directly from a delftware 'blue-dash' dish (see page 100). The same style of pottery was still being made locally in Pennsylvania in the early nineteenth century. In fact, *sgraffiato* wares were never to reach a position of predominance, and as in Italy from the seventeenth century onwards, their rôle was universally to be that of a 'peasant' ware, much of which was made to commemorate personal or family events such as births or marriages. Such pottery is still made today in many places, much of it to satisfy the tourist market.

English 'Tudor' and 'Cistercian' wares

The coloured lead-glazed wares of sixteenth-century Europe present some strange contrasts. The potters of Tudor England appear to have been struck by a wave of almost fanatical austerity and produced vessels of simple form, largely cups and jugs, usually of a buff clay covered with a deep, copper-green glaze. The same demand for simplicity was to be seen in the contemporary 'Malling' tin-glazed jugs (see page 98). Probably in the latter part of the sixteenth century began the manufacture of pottery made of a dark red body covered with a deep brown, almost black, glaze. As a group these wares were first recognized from the ruins of Cistercian abbeys in northern England abolished in the 1530s, and the name 'Cistercian' is often applied to them. On the other hand, the same type of pottery was being made in Staffordshire, at Burslem for example, in the first half of the seventh century. The shapes produced were to be copied extensively in the seventeenth century: straight-sided mugs and beakers with flaring rims, provided with two, three or more handles, often quaintly called 'tygs', were to become common vessels decorated in slip (see page 125) and to a lesser extent provided the inspiration for some delftwares.

Sauce-boat in coloured earthenware by Palissy, c. 1580.

Bernard Palissy and St Porchaire

The sixteenth century in France saw the emergence and
eclipse of two very different types of lead-glazed ware. The
one was a flamboyant style created by Bernard Palissy, who
was born near Agen in about 1510. In 1539 he settled in
Saintes (see page 59) where he painted on glass and experimented with coloured glazes. In 1563 he set up a workshop
at the Tuileries in Paris. As a Protestant his survival was
assured by his patron, Catherine de Médicis, but on her death
in 1588 he was flung into the Bastille, where he died the following year. Palissy is usually remembered for his elaborately
moulded wares in which snakes, fish and shells were cast
from actual specimens and coloured in true-to-life glazes.
Examples of his work were clearly made from casts of contemporary metalwork of which one, depicting a reclining
nude, *Fecundity*, was later extensively copied in English
delftware. By contrast, the potteries of St Porchaire, at no
great distance from Saintes, between the years 1530 and 1570
were producing a crisp white earthenware decorated in red
and black underglaze slips.

Small lead-glazed jug from London
(*right*), *c.* 1500; and a three-
handled beaker from Burslem (*left*),
c. 1650.

The Preunings of Nuremberg

Palissy and the unknown potters of St Porchaire were isolated phenomena. Elsewhere in France vessels covered with poly-chrome glazes, many being direct copies of metal types, were made throughout the late sixteenth and seventeenth centuries. In Germany this kind of pottery seems to have been pioneered by the Preuning family of Nuremberg, whose earliest products date from the second quarter of the sixteenth century, although the origins have sometimes erroneously been attributed to the almost legendary Hirschvogels in the opening years of the century. Many of their wares show zones or friezes of figures in relief set against a deep cobalt blue background. Popular subjects were Biblical or mythological scenes, and there is a very obvious stylistic interdependence between the Preuning earthenwares and the 'enamelled' stonewares of contemporary Kreussen (see page 114), the cobalt blue glaze of the one performing the same functions as the black slip of the other. These wares were copied with success both at Krems in Austria, and at Annaberg in Saxony. Although the Preunings continued to make this ware to the end of the seventeenth century, its production thereafter fell to the level of a 'peasant' craft, in which guise it is still to be found in various localities today.

European slipwares

Like the *sgraffiato* wares, the slip-decorated wares of Europe have received little systematic study. Amongst the earliest European potteries to produce these wares were those of Wanfried-an-der-Werra in Hesse, which began production in the late sixteenth century. The wares were a red earthenware with designs piped in white clay and covered with a lead glaze which was sometimes stained green with copper. Both figure and geometric motifs were used, and the pottery was traded largely to Friesland, but also to England. In the sixteenth and seventeenth centuries the technique was used widely in small European potteries, especially to produce commemorative mugs and dishes, and at some potteries, as for example Krefeld (see page 121), slip-trailing and *sgraffiato* decoration were used side by side, or even together on the same vessel. The earliest slip-trailed wares in England were

Jug in coloured earthenware (*bottom*), by the Preunings of Nuremberg, *c.* 1560 and slipware dish from Wanfried-an-der-Werra, dated 1615.

those made at Wrotham in Kent from the opening decade of the seventeenth century, where decoration was applied to the typical 'Cistercian' forms (see page 122). At much the same time a second pottery, probably at Harlow in Essex, was producing similar wares, usually known as 'Metropolitan' slipware, in which pious inscriptions, such as HONOUR THE LORD, or FEAR GOD, were favoured motifs.

Slipware dish by Samuel Malkin of Burslem, *c.* 1730.

Staffordshire slipwares

Staffordshire slip decoration reached its height with the work
of Thomas and Ralph Toft whose dishes, often approaching
two feet in diameter, bear dates ranging from 1671 to 1689.
These were made of red earthenware, the face of which was
covered with white slip and on which designs were carried
out in red and dark brown clays, the whole surface finally
being lead-glazed. Commonly figures would be outlined in
dark brown and filled in with red slip, while the dark outline
was further emphasized by being picked out with a series of
white dots – a technique that was, curiously, also used by a
small group of ninth-century potters making 'Samarquand'
wares (see page 35). Motifs include 'The Pelican in her Piety',
mermaids and portraits, as well as 'Adam and Eve'. The use of
freely trailed slip as a means of decorating large dishes gave
way in the 1720s to a system in which the wares were press-
moulded and in which the design was partly recessed to receive
areas of coloured slip.

'Marbled' and 'feathered' slipware

As by-products of the slip-trailing technique there evolved two other methods of decoration achieved by manipulating slips on the rather damp surface of partly dried wares. In the one, horizontal bands of differently coloured slips were laid down, and while still wet, a point was drawn at right-angles across the bands, so dragging the slip into a 'feather' pattern. In the other, areas of bands of coloured slip were laid on, and the whole vessel was joggled in such a way that the slips produced the whorled pattern of marble. Both techniques were used sparingly on slip-trailed wares in England from the early seventeenth century, ultimately to become the most widespread of all 'peasant' decorative techniques in the late eighteenth and nineteenth centuries, not only in England, but throughout Europe. Both 'marbling' and 'feathering' are frequently to be seen on English utilitarian wares, such as mugs and oven dishes of the nineteenth century, while Bernard Leach (see page 148) and other English potters have revived the method within this century.

Slipware dish with marbled effect. Probably Staffordshire, *c.* 1800.

FINE WHITE EARTHENWARE
Staffordshire earthenwares

The first half of the eighteenth century was a critical period in the development of Staffordshire pottery. One can, nevertheless, trace the stages by which Staffordshire rose to supremacy in the manufacture of earthenware during the period from 1710 to 1780. The year 1710 is taken as a starting-point, for it was then that the Elers Brothers (see page 117) left Staffordshire; that delftware began to be made in Liverpool (see page 108); and the last year in which the great hand-trailed slipware dishes in the Toft manner (see page 126) were produced. The next twenty years saw a limited range of earthenware which included a 'dry' red and a 'dry' black body – the same body, the latter darkened by additions of iron carstone from coalmines – and 'dry' buff and chocolate brown bodies. Decoration was confined largely to applied 'sprigs' in the same material as the body or to slip-trailing in white pipe-clay. Traditionally attributed to John Astbury, the sprig-moulded wares were clearly being made by many other Staffordshire potters, including Thomas Wedgwood (see page 116).

Roumanian jug in trailed slip decoration c. 1800; Staffordshire cream jug c. 1750 and (*opposite*) teapot with white sprigged decoration, Staffordshire, about 1740.

Staffordshire creamwares

In the 1730s the Astburys produced a red or buff earthenware sprig-moulded in white. Much of this ware was made to commemorate the capture of Porto Bello in 1739, and it is often known by this name. At much the same time Thomas Wedgwood began the production of an agate ware. The most significant development of the decade, however, was the introduction of an off-white body. It has already been seen how Thomas Astbury had perfected a white stoneware body (see page 118). The same body covered with a lead glaze, and fired to a lower temperature than the stoneware, gave a deep cream-coloured ware. In this early form the ware had many defects. The glaze, still applied as a powder, had many irregularities, while the colour was variable in tone and in no way approached the whiteness of stoneware or delftware, still less that of porcelain, to which end the potters had set their caps. Even so, as a raw material it had potential advantages. It was cheap to produce; it was less liable to chip than delftware; and unlike the stonewares its surface was not so hard that it abraided silver cutlery. By the early 1740s many Staffordshire potters had begun to produce, and experiment with creamwares.

Booth, Wedgwood and Whieldon: improved lead glazes

In the decade following 1740 great improvements were made in the quality of lead glazes, innovations which were attributed to Enoch Booth of Tunstall, Aaron Wedgwood of Burslem, and Thomas Whieldon of Fenton Low. Briefly, the lead ore was ground under water with calcined flint and pipe-clay, and applied as a suspension to the green-hard shapes – an introduction attributed to Wedgwood. To Booth is given the credit for applying the suspension to wares already fired (biscuit), requiring a second firing to form the glaze; while Whieldon is said to have replaced the pipe-clay. Both Booth and Wedgwood at times counter-tinted their glazes with cobalt, the blue of which to a degree 'killed' the cream colour of the iron impurities. The Staffordshire potters thus had a creamware of a quality which could begin to compete with its rivals and on which decoration could be carried out either in the newly acquired 'enamels' (see page 119) or by using coloured glazes. Whieldon further developed the 'agate' wares of Thomas Wedgwood by staining some of the batches of clay used in the body with cobalt and manganese.

Tea caddy in agate ware.
Whieldon, c. 1750.
(*opposite*) Tea caddy and plate with printed decoration.
Wedgwood, c. 1770.

Sadler and Green: transfer-printing

Having overcome the problem of producing an economical creamware, the Staffordshire potters of the 1750s were evidently faced with yet another obstacle, that of providing polychrome decoration. The underglaze colours as used in Whieldon's agate wares were clearly too restricting. On the other hand, to employ 'enamellers' was expensive. One obvious answer was to print the enamels on to the surface. Basically what was evolved was a technique in which the engraved lines of a copper plate were filled with finely powdered enamel colours and a suitable printer's ink. The pattern was then printed on to a piece of paper and transferred to the surface of the ware. Much of the development of transfer-printing was pioneered by the Battersea Enamel Works between 1753 and 1756 where a hairless paper, a suitable etching technique and a printer's ink had to be evolved to make the process viable. Despite the fact that these problems were overcome, the company failed, but in the same year, 1756, John Sadler began commercial production in Liverpool, and in 1763 went into partnership with Guy Green. At first Sadler printed only in black, but after his partnership with Green, other colours – red, purple and brown – were developed.

Teapot with crabstock handle. Whieldon, *c*. 1770.

(*opposite*) Coffee-pot imitating a cauliflower. Wedgwood, *c*. 1760.

Whieldon: coloured lead glazes

Thomas Whieldon was born in 1719. By 1740 he was an established master-potter and the first to produce creamware in any quantity, and although he produced the whole range of glazed and unglazed wares, his work shows a leaning towards the use of coloured glazes in conjunction with the creamware body. In its most elaborate form, powdered colours were dabbed on in patches under the lead glaze: cobalt, manganese, copper and iron ores were used in this way to give a mottled or 'tortoiseshell' effect. Equally, Whieldon was content to work with coloured glazes applied as areas on the surface of his wares – a technique seen at its best when used with relief decoration of leaves, fruit, flowers and vegetables, the leaves picked out in green, and the flowers and fruit in other colours. To such wares were usually applied rusticated or 'crabstock' handles, spouts and knobs, modelled in the form of twigs. A large part of Whieldon's success lay in his ability to pick men of genius as his modellers. Two such men were Aaron Wood (1717–1785) and William Greatbach, both of whom later worked for Josiah Wedgwood, while another was Josiah Spode.

Josiah Wedgwood: the early period

Josiah Wedgwood, a grandson of the Thomas Wedgwood alluded to earlier (see pages 116 and 128), was born in 1730. In 1752 Josiah set up on his own, but two years later, at the age of twenty-four, he was taken into partnership by Thomas Whieldon. In Wedgwood's own phrase, 'something new was wanted to give a little spirit to the business', which explains why Whieldon was prepared to enter into partnership with so young a man. The 'something new' was research into coloured glazes, and in 1759 a greatly improved green glaze was produced, followed a year later by a clear yellow one. The partnership ended in 1759 and Wedgwood set up on his own again at the Ivy House works, moving five years later to the Brick House, Burslem. Before this move, Wedgwood's products are on the whole indistinguishable from those of Whieldon, for he made the same range of wares, including jugs and teapots modelled in the form of pineapples and cauliflowers embellished with his green and yellow glazes. By 1762 he was so confident in his ability to produce a consistently coloured ware, that he presented a 'breakfast set' to Queen Charlotte, and in 1765 referred to his creamware as 'Queen's Ware'.

Vegetable dish in Queen's Ware. Wedgwood, *c.* 1780.

Josiah Wedgwood: the later period

In 1760 began a working agreement with John Sadler (see page 131) in which wares were sent from Burslem to Liverpool to be transfer-printed. In spite of the fact that Wedgwood insisted upon approving the designs and the colours and insisted on patterns exclusive to his own products, it was not until 1784 that he set up his own printing shop. Of far greater importance was the partnership entered into with Thomas Bentley of Chelsea, in 1770, as an outcome of which wares were sent to London, there to be 'enamelled' by hand. Under this partnership was produced one of the greatest sales promotions of all time, the Imperial Russian Service, completed in 1775. Containing 952 items, the initial cost was a little over £50, but by the time each item had been decorated with an English landscape scene, none being repeated, the cost had risen to £3,500. Painted in a dingy purple its only claim to credit lay in the custom it brought the partnership, for by now Wedgwood had abandoned the earlier rustic and *chinoiserie* styles and was producing creamwares in the severe shapes of Neo-Classicism, in which decoration was largely confined to simple leaf or Greek-derived borders.

Josiah Wedgwood: 'basaltes' and other dry bodies

Although Wedgwood must be remembered primarily for enhancing and promoting creamwares, he also inherited other Staffordshire wares which he improved. The 'Egyptian' black of the Astbury-Whieldon period was reformulated in 1779 using the finer Devonshire clays in place of local ones, manganese was added, and the iron-bearing carstone was refined. This gave a dense, truly black body, which he renamed 'basaltes'. Similarly, Wedgwood further refined the dark and light red and the buff bodies to re-christen them 'rosso antico', 'terra cotta' and 'cane' wares. These dry bodies, especially the 'basaltes' were used largely for cameos, ornamental vases, busts and other decorative goods, for the manufacture of which Wedgwood built a separate workshop which he named 'Etruria', but he also made useful wares of the same materials, rendering them impervious by glazing the inner surfaces. These wares were often decorated in relief, while the 'cane' body was not infrequently used to simulate bamboo. Many of these wares, too, were turned on a 'rose-engine', a lathe with an eccentrically mounted cutting-head capable of producing patterns similar to those made by a 'spirograph'. This device was also used by Whieldon and John Turner of Lane End, for example.

Coffee-pot in basaltes ware. Wedgwood, c. 1780.

Josiah Wedgwood: 'jasper' ware

The third major group of wares produced by Wedgwood depended upon his development from 1774 onwards of a truly white body that could be made to take up an even colouring of green, yellow, lilac and black, although variations in firing might produce other shades such as sage-green, pink, or coffee brown. To the coloured body were applied white reliefs to provide a cameo effect. In the early years the material was used entirely for making small decorative objects and it was only after 1780 that Wedgwood had sufficiently mastered it to be able to make larger objects. Even then it was used mostly for the production of decorative vases, of which the copy of the Roman cameo-glass masterpiece, the 'Portland' vase (1790), was the most remarkable. Coffee-pots and teapots, jugs, cups and saucers were made in this 'jasper' ware and were copied by other Staffordshire potters, most successfully by John Turner and William Adams. Turner specialized in a green 'jasper' and Adams in a body that was violet. Jasper ware, however, was always a luxury product, and was never as widely made in Staffordshire as the other wares pioneered by Wedgwood and his contemporaries.

Urn and teapot in 'jasper' ware. Wedgwood, *c.* 1780.

Wedgwood's contemporaries: Leeds, Liverpool and Bristol

The main rival to the Staffordshire potteries was Leeds, where a factory had been established in the 1750s. Although other common Staffordshire wares were made, Leeds became renowned for its creamware, made by the Brothers Green at their factory at Hunslet. The ware itself was yellower than that of Staffordshire, and the glaze tended to be faintly green. In the early years much of the ware was decorated by a Leeds firm of enamellers, Robinson and Rhodes, who operated between 1760 and 1768. In 1775 William Hartley, an astute businessman, joined the firm, and during the period of his partnership its trade expanded and it absorbed a number of local workshops, chiefly the Swinton and Don potteries. By 1780 Leeds had begun to do its own transfer-printing, and three years later, following the lead given by Wedgwood, a catalogue was issued and the wares were marked. A less important centre of creamware manufacture was that of Liverpool where the Herculaneum factory was set up in 1796. In Bristol creamware began to be made rather earlier – from about 1785 onwards. Herculaneum wares are greyer than those of Leeds and Staffordshire; those of Bristol have a yellow glaze on an almost white body.

Enamelled plate and teapot. Leeds, *c.* 1770.

Wedgwood's contemporaries: Ralph Wood and Felix Pratt

The main exponent of the Whieldon tradition (see page 132) was Ralph Wood (1715–1772), who was to become the Staffordshire fun-potter, and who introduced figure jugs, of which the so-called 'Toby' is the best known, although many other caricatures were made. Made in multi-piece moulds, the jugs were decorated in a limited range of brown, blue, green and purple glazes. After Wood's death, his son Ralph Wood II, continued to make these wares, being joined in 1783 by his cousin, Enoch Wood. From about 1790, however, gaudy overglaze 'enamels' began to be used and modelling became peremptory, while Enoch turned his attention to other Staffordshire wares, including underglaze blue printed goods (see page 140). From about 1790 many craftsmen in Staffordshire and elsewhere made pottery decorated in low relief, coloured with underglaze ochre, blue, green, brown and purple. This type of decoration is traditionally attributed to Felix Pratt (1780–1859) of Fenton. Hunting and domestic scenes were the common motifs of relief decoration, while in some potteries the underglaze colours were used alone in floral painting. Production lingered on into the 1830s.

Lustreware cup and jug. Staffordshire, c. 1820.

Toby jug by Ralph Wood, c. 1770: tea caddy by Felix Pratt, c. 1780.

English lustre and 'mocha' wares

The opening decade of the nineteenth century saw the introduction of lustres. Essentially there were two types: one, based upon platinum, gave a 'silver' lustre when applied to a creamware body; the other, based on gold, gave a pink or purple lustre when applied to a creamware or white-slipped surface, and a 'copper' lustre when put down on a red body or slip. 'Silver' lustre was often used all over a creamware shape to imitate contemporary silverwares; while the purple lustres were frequently applied to creamwares as a marbling or mottling. From about 1820 'copper' lustre was often used in conjunction with relief decoration. A second decorative technique that became popular in the opening years of the nineteenth century was that of 'mocha' ware, in which an infusion of tobacco was mixed with an underglaze pigment, and a drop of this concoction was allowed to 'crawl' over the green-hard surface to make a fern or moss-like pattern. 'Mocha' decoration was widely used on jugs, bowls and mugs from the early nineteenth century.

THE INDUSTRIAL AGE
Staffordshire underglaze printing

A system of transfer-printing in blue, to be used under the glaze, was developed in the 1760s, probably by the ill-fated Battersea Enamel Works (see page 131). It was further improved upon by Robert Hancock at Worcester and Thomas Turner of Caughley, both of whom were applying the technique to porcelain. Shortly after 1780, Thomas Turner and Josiah Spode were making creamware decorated in underglaze transfer-printed blue. By 1830 some two hundred Staffordshire potters were producing underglaze printed wares of this kind, usually in blue, but also in black, sepia, red, green or purple. Initially patterns were adaptations of Chinese porcelains, or even deliberately-created *chinoiseries*, of which the 'willow pattern', introduced by Turner in 1780, became the most popular of all. Underglaze printing was ideally suited to industrialized production, and by 1840 nearly every country in Europe as well as the newly established American Pottery Company of New Jersey (see page 143), was making its own versions of underglaze printed pottery.

'Indian tree' and 'willow pattern'; two popular designs in underglaze printing introduced in 1801 and 1780.

(*opposite*) Multi-coloured printed plate after an engraving by Jesse Austin. Pratt, *c.* 1850.

Multi-colour printing

By the 1840s at least two Staffordshire firms, including Collins & Reynolds of Hanley, and Pratt of Fenton, were experimenting with full polychrome printing. The latter were the more successful of the two, thanks largely to the work of their engraver, Jesse Austin, who by 1848 had perfected a system of superimposing five or more differently coloured transfers. The process, as can be imagined, called for considerable skill and ingenuity on the part of the engravers, some printing plates being executed in a stipple and others in a line technique. A large part of the early output was devoted not to table and decorative earthenwares, but to the lids of pots destined to contain fish-paste, pomade or macassar oil, a number of manufacturers being quick to realize the value of these gaily coloured lids in promoting sales. Subject-matter varied enormously, from pictures of bears, advertising bear's grease, to seascapes, advertising fish-paste. Tablewares in multi-colour printing, often copying paintings by Landseer or Gainsborough, were usually of soft-paste porcelain and not of earthenware.

Apostle jug in slip-cast
stoneware. Charles Meigh,
c. 1850.
(*opposite*) Jug with
Rockingham glaze.
Jersey City, *c.* 1840.

Slip-cast stonewares

From the 1830s began the manufacture of highly ornamental
stonewares decorated in relief, chiefly jugs, teapots and mugs.
This revival is usually associated with the work of Charles
Meigh of Hanley, who produced large numbers of white,
unglazed, slip-cast jugs in the 'Gothic' style, most notably a
straight-sided jug with an ornate handle and decorated with a
frieze of Apostles each standing within a lancet arch. Other
potters, as for example Minton of Stoke, produced similar
wares frequently decorated with a sprawling pattern of
foliage, the stems of which originated from a 'rustic' handle.
The same genre of design is to be found on red salt-glazed wares
of the mid-century, more often than not with hideous results.
An exception could be made for this class of ware at Beauvais
(see page 121), where, under the influence of Jules-Claude
Ziegler, running-plant patterns were used on salt-glaze
stoneware with considerably greater restraint. Shortly before
the mid-century a number of potteries were being established
in the United States (see page 143), and it was this style of
decoration, although largely applied to earthenwares, that
was to dominate early production in the New World.

'Rockingham' glazes and *émaux ombrants*

Usually applied to a cane-coloured body, the 'Rockingham' glaze had been used to decorate teapots, jugs and kitchen utensils by many small potters from the early nineteenth century. By the mid-century the glaze was being used in conjunction with relief decoration of the type described on page 142, a style that was to dominate early American production. In 1849 a patent for a type of Rockingham glaze was taken out by C. W. Fenton of Bennington, Vermont (the United States Pottery Company), while wares of the same type were made in quantity by E. and W. Bennett of Baltimore, the American Pottery Company of New Jersey, Taylor & Speeler of Trenton, and at East Liverpool, Ohio. Of a rather different order was a style of decoration evolved by Baron du Tremblay at Rubelles near Melun in the 1840s. An impressed relief decoration was covered with a clear-coloured glaze, which 'pooled' into the deeper recesses to provide varying shades of colour. Called by the French '*émail ombrant*', the technique has a close parallel in metal enamelling, *basse taille*, although when used with a green glaze the results have a passing similarity to some of the poorer quality celadons (see page 38).

The Exhibition Age

The pottery industry suffered more than most from the Exhibition Mania, which had begun after the Paris Exhibition of 1844. Encouraged always to provide 'something new' and their ideas often plagiarized, they had to beg, borrow and steal more often than in all the preceding millennia. The beginnings of this *malaise* can be seen in the 1840s in Britain with the production of extremely weak copies of Greek red-figure wares (see page 17) made by Dillwyns of Swansea. This style of work, then believed to be 'Etruscan', was imitated by a number of Staffordshire potters, and even translated into blue-and-white versions. At the same time in France, Charles Avisseau of Tours began to copy, with far greater success, the work of Bernard Palissy (see page 123). At least two potteries in Paris followed this lead, and the style was in turn adopted by Mafra & Son of Caldas da Rainha in Portugal and by Minton of Stoke. Other French potters copied the wares of St Porchaire (see page 123), then known as 'Henry Deux', a style also seized upon by Minton, at that time directed by the Frenchman, Léon Arnoux.

'Majolica'

In the 1850s Ristori of Nevers made good copies of Italian tin-glazed wares. These styles were soon taken up by Italian potters themselves in Rome, Doccia and Florence – most successfully by Ulysse Cantagalli of Florence (see page 82). Italian 'Majolica', as it was then known, was further copied in the Berlin State Porcelain Factory and again by Minton. The term 'Majolica', however, rapidly changed its original, narrow meaning and came to be applied to creamwares decorated in coloured glazes, usually heavily decorated in relief, frequently with an excessive use of gilding. In this sense 'Majolica' was to become one of the major items of pottery production in the late Victorian world, by which time it bore little or no relationship to the original Italian tin-glazed wares. Dissatisfaction with these purely imitative styles led a number of manufacturers into various arrangements with artists. Henry Cole (under the pseudonym, Felix Summerly) provided a body of artists, the Art Manufacturers, to turn out suitable designs. However, such arrangements were seldom successful.

Hop jug designed by Henry Townsend. Minton, *c.* 1860. and (*above*) vase imitating St Porchaire wares. Minton, *c.* 1890.

Early 'studio' pottery

The origin of 'studio' pottery – the Movement in which there was a return to the idea of the designer being both potter and artist – can be traced to the work of Théodore Deck, whose early work in earthenware was greatly influenced by Iznik and Persian wares. The same influences are to be seen in the earthenwares of William De Morgan, who was a close associate of William Morris and particularly concerned with the production of lustrewares in the 1880s. Lustre-decorated earthenware was to become very popular amongst European artist-potters at the turn of the century as shown, for example, in the work of Clément Massier of Golfe-Juan, near Cannes; the von Heiders of Schongau, Bavaria, and Herman Kähler of Naestved, Denmark. In France, artist-potters, following the lead given by Deck, tended to work in porcelain or stoneware, and it was in the 1870s that 'Japanese' motifs were first applied to these bodies. By the 1880s attention had turned equally to the heavy flowing glazes on Japanese tea-bowls and jars, which were extensively copied and adapted to stonewares by French artist-potters such as Auguste Delaherche and Jean Carriès or the German, Julius Scharvogel of Munich.

Art Nouveau

In 1887 a Japanese potter, Kataro Shirayamadani joined the staff of the Rookwood Pottery, founded by Mrs Maria Nichols in 1880 in Cincinnati, Ohio, in a converted school. In 1890 Mrs Nichols turned the concern over to her manager, William N. Taylor. Using various combinations of coloured body, slip and glaze, particularly brilliant effects were achieved. First attracting attention at the Paris Exhibition of 1889, Rookwood pottery was awarded the *Grand Prix* at Paris in 1900. The pottery was, of course, in the distinctive and immediately recognizable category of *Art Nouveau*, but examination of the Rookwood wares shows just what a composite style this was. The forms, largely jugs and vases, derive from T'ang and Sung wares; the decoration derives from Japan; while the technology is entirely Western, particularly where combined with copper and silver electroplating, or the use of crystalline and matt glazes. In this specific case the contributions made by Kataro Shirayamadani and William N. Taylor are immediately discernible.

Bernard Leach

Bernard Leach, although born in China, was educated in England. After leaving the Slade School of Art he taught in Japan where he learnt the traditional local methods of making pottery. In 1920 he returned to England to establish his own workshop at St Ives in Cornwall, accompanied by the Japanese potter, Shoji Hamada. Broadly speaking, Leach chose not to emulate any one particular style, but rather what he personally felt to be the most enduring qualities in pottery from many places and ages, which he incorporated in his own work. Relying entirely upon local raw materials and using the wheel as a means of shaping, in most of his work can be seen the influence of Sung (see page 36) and traditional English forms, while the rather sober decoration reflects equally the freedom of line of Tz'u-chou painted (see page 42) and English slip-trailed wares (see page 126). Leach's influence, however, was to reach far beyond his own students, all of whom, as was proper, selected their own set of ceramic qualities as guides.

Stoneware dish. Bernard Leach.

The designer in industry

During the early decade of the twentieth century, as the Studio Pottery Movement gathered momentum, industrial pottery suffered a period of indecision that amounted at times to schizophrenia. Many industrialists firmly believed that their function was to imitate the old, and that it was essential to disguise the industrial origin of their wares, but others, more adventurous, followed the fashions set by the studio-potters and translated hand-made wares into the medium of mass-production. In neither case, however, were the goods specifically designed for machine manufacture. By the 1920s, the 'functionalism', propounded by Walter Gropius, resulted in the general acceptance that machine-made goods demanded their own design. On the Continent of Europe 'functional' designs were largely applied to porcelain, but in Britain, Keith Murray, working for Wedgwood & Sons in the 1930s, produced simply-designed wares, that were to become one of many starting-points in the development of pottery created unashamedly with mechanical production in mind.

Vase designed by Keith Murray. Wedgwood, 1935.

Kitchen-dining-room wares

The trend towards living in flats and smaller houses, and the disappearance of the domestic servant, have naturally obliterated the rigid distinction between kitchen and dining-room wares, at least for daily use. The development in the 1930s of oven-proof glassware that could be brought directly to table opened a new field for stonewares and other heat-proof bodies. Amongst the pioneers in this style of pottery were the firms of Arabia in Finland, and Joseph Bourne of Denby. The 'Kilta' wares, designed for Arabia by Kaj Frank, who has also worked in glass and textiles, illustrate even further how modern living conditions can impose upon design, for not only are the wares heat-proof, but as was previously the case only in oven-proof glassware, the lids of casseroles, for example, can be used equally as shallow dishes. Further concessions to the small house with its lack of storage space are to be seen in the elimination of protruding handles that prevent vessels from being stacked within one another, or the ubiquitous straight-sided cup with a narrower cylindrical foot that allows several cups to be piled safely upon one another. A wide range of these vessels can be used together, or in conjunction with hand-made pottery of the same genre of colouring, without producing too discordant a result.

Plastic teacup and saucer and milk jug.

Stainless steel and plastics: 'uni-design'

In its long history, pottery has frequently been influenced by other materials (see pages 26, 28, 31, 81 and 112), and there is bound to be a wide variety of functions which vessels made of stainless steel, plastics and pottery share in common and in which one would expect to see great similarity of design. One must be less happy, however, when one finds features adopted by potters that make sense only when used with some other material. Thus, in the making of a plastic jug or cup the handle will have to be cast in one with the vessel, since it cannot be stuck on afterwards. It is an equal absurdity to design a plastic cup with a handle that looks as though it had been applied, as it is to produce one in pottery with a handle that suggests it was cast in one with the vessel. By the same token, a stainless steel kettle may be designed with as broad a base as possible to ensure maximum heating efficiency, but there seems little point in translating this form into ceramics and calling it a 'teapot'. The criteria by which today's industrial pottery will be judged in the future will be the same as those by which all pottery should be judged: its fitness to fulfil its function within the context of its own time.

Peasant pottery today

Truly peasant pottery today is hard to find, and many crafts-men, who even a decade ago made wares to be used locally, have turned their hands to the more profitable tourist market with its very different demands. Little could be more bizarre than the products of one potter in western Anatolia who makes copies of tall Roman wine-jars which are daubed with plaster, pebbles and sea-shells, and sold as antiques dredged from some ancient wreck. Nor has commercialism been the only source of undoing, for in those countries where peasant crafts have been lauded as the only true arts of the people, the careful fostering by the State has usually resulted in a 're-introduction' of 'traditional' designs, an academic nurtur-ing that has normally engendered something that is neither peasant nor studio pottery. There remain, however, an ever-decreasing number of regions in which the tourist or the inspector for local crafts would be received as curiosities, and here one will find the local potters making honest, functional goods for their neighbours. Their materials and techniques will reflect, more likely than not, an echo of some past golden age, as too may their decoration.

Primitive pottery today

Although most primitive pottery is simple and utilitarian, this is not invariably the case, as illustrated, for example, by the Nazca and Mochica wares made in Peru during the early centuries of our era. Made in moulds, their jugs in the form of animals or figures, often show not only a high technical ability, but also a developed sense of caricature. Although primitive vessels have inspired modern studio-potters, removed from their own social context, they must necessarily lose the larger part of their relevance, and the wares they inspire can be little better than mechanical copies. Indeed, what has already been said about peasant pottery is equally true of primitive wares. A cooking-pot sitting in a museum showcase may tell us a great deal about its makers, about their way of life, or even their artistic heritage. Alas, the same cooking-pot, or a copy, removed to an all-electric kitchen, tells us something about our own society. Acquisitive and eclectic, we have not yet come to terms with the machine and mass-production. A yearning for something that is, or looks, hand-made, reflects our doubts. As always, so today, the pottery we use in the home is a mirror of our age.

Polychrome painted vase. Peru.
(*opposite*) Modern peasant pottery. Poland.

GLOSSARY

Alkali, a caustic material, usually either soda or potash

Alkaline glaze, a glaze in which the silica is fluxed with an alkali

Ash glaze, a glaze in which both the silica and fluxes are derived from plant or wood ashes

Biscuit (or Bisque), a ware that has been fired prior to glazing

Body, the material from which pottery is made. Usually a mixture of clay and other minerals (fillers)

Chipping, the tendency for a glaze to peel away from the body

Combing, a decorative technique in which a comb is dragged across the damp surface of a vessel so producing a feather-like pattern

Clay, a natural mineral, an alumina silicate, made up of very small particles, but often containing other impurities

Crackle (Crazing), the tendency for a glaze to develop hair-like cracks like a fine net on the surface

Creamware, an off-white earthenware body covered with a lead glaze developed in Staffordshire in the eighteenth century

Dipping, the usual way of applying a slip or glaze by immersion in a vat

Earthenware, a body that fires below 1200°C. Usually coloured red or cream, invariably porous

Enamels, colours made of a glaze with a low melting point, applied to glazed wares and fired in a second firing

Faïence, Italian tin-glazed wares of the Renaissance. The term is also used to describe later European wares of the same type

Felspar, a natural mineral containing a high proportion of alkalis

Fettling, the general tidying-up given to pottery after it has been shaped and allowed to dry

Filler, a material added to clay to form the body from which pottery is made. Usually sand or crushed rock

Flux, a material that will lower the melting-point of silica and make it flow readily. Usually an alkali or a compound of lead

Frit, glaze materials that have been fused and then powdered

Gloss, the very fine slip found on classical Greek and Samian wares

Glost, a second firing given to pottery to form the glaze

Hard glaze, a hard glaze fired at a high temperature. Usually an alkaline glaze

Kiln, a device in which pottery is fired

Lead glaze, a glaze in which the main flux is a compound of lead

Lustre, a thin metallic coating lying over the glazed surface

Luting, joining unfired parts of a vessel using slip as adhesive

Majolica, the name given to Spanish lustrewares by the Italians

Modelling, shaping damp clay with fingers or tools

Moulding, shaping damp clay by pressing into a mould of the required form

Muffle, a wall inside a kiln that prevents the flames of the fire making direct contact with the wares

Overglaze, colours applied to the surface of a ware after it has been glazed

Oxidation, a smoke-free firing that allows plenty of air into the kiln

Potash, a common alkali present in wood ash, saltpetre and some felspars

Quartz, a rock composed of silica

Reduction, a smoke-laden firing in which little air enters the kiln

Saggar, an abbreviation of 'safeguard'. A clay box in which glazed wares are fired to keep them away from the flame

Salt glaze, an alkaline glaze in which soda is obtained by throwing salt on the kiln fire

Sgraffiato, a decorative technique in which the design is scratched through a slip

Shrinking, all wares shrink on drying and again on firing

Silica, the oxide of silicon. The most common mineral of the earth's crust

Slip, clay mixed with water: a layer of this material applied to the surfaces of a vessel

Slip-trailing, clay applied through a nozzle as one might ice a cake

Soda, a common alkali present in nitre and washing soda

Soft glaze, a soft glaze fired at a low temperature, usually a lead glaze

Sprigging, a decorative technique in which motifs are formed in small moulds and stuck on the surface of wares

Stonewares, bodies that fire between 1150° and 1300°C. Usually of a pale colour, invariably non-porous

Terracotta, earthenware bodies fired below 900°C. Red, soft and very porous

Throwing, shaping pottery on a wheel that is rotating rapidly

Tin glaze, a dense white glaze made by adding tin oxide to a lead glaze

Transfer-printing, applying a printed design to the surface of a ware by means of a strip of transfer paper

Turning, shaving down the surface of a vessel after it has dried either on a potter's wheel or on a lathe

Underglaze, colours applied to the surface of a ware before it has been glazed

BOOKS TO READ

There are many monographs dealing with limited aspects of the history of pottery, some relating only to the products of a single workshop. The books mentioned here are of a more general nature.

The Art of the Potter by W. B. Honey. Faber, London, 1946.

The Ceramic Art of China and Other Countries of the Far East by W. B. Honey. Faber, London, 1945.

La Céramique Française by G. Fontaine. Larousse, Paris, 1965.

English Pottery and Porcelain by W. B. Honey, (6th Ed.). A. & C. Black, London, 1969.

Five Centuries of Italian Majolica by G. Liverani. McGraw-Hill, London, 1960.

Hafner und Hafnerhandwerk in Südwestdeutschland by G. Spies. Tübingen, 1964.

Iranian Ceramics by C. K. Wilkinson. Abrams, New York, 1963.

Lustreware of Spain by Alice W. Frothingham. Hispanic Society of America, New York, 1951.

A Potter's Book by B. Leach. Faber, London, 1945.

Pottery through the Ages by G. Savage. Penguin, London, 1959.

Style in Pottery by A. Lane. Oxford University Press, London, 1948.

World Ceramics edited by R. J. Charleston. Paul Hamlyn, London, 1968.

PLACES TO VISIT
In Britain

Nearly every museum, no matter how small, displays a collection of pottery. The museums listed here have large, comprehensive collections.

The British Museum, London
The Victoria and Albert Museum, London
The Percival David Foundation, London
Guildhall Museum, London
The City Museum, Stoke-on-Trent
The Ashmolean Museum, Oxford
The Fitzwilliam Museum, Cambridge

In America

Cincinnati Art Museum, Cincinnati
Cleveland Museum of Art, Ohio
Metropolitan Museum of Art, New York
Museum of Fine Arts, Boston
Newark Museum, New Jersey
Seattle Art Museum, Seattle
Smithsonian Institution, Washington

INDEX

SOME OTHER TITLES IN THIS SERIES

■ Arts
■ Domestic Animals and Pets
■ Domestic Science
■ Gardening

■ General Information
■ History and Mythology
■ Natural History
■ Popular Science

Arts
Antique Furniture/Architecture/Clocks and Watches/Glass for Collectors/Jewellery/Musical Instruments/Porcelain/Pottery/Victoriana

Domestic Animals and Pets
Budgerigars/Cats/Dog Care/Dogs/Horses and Ponies/Pet Birds/Pets for Children/Tropical Freshwater Aquaria/Tropical Marine Aquaria

Domestic Science
Flower Arranging

Gardening
Chrysanthemums/Garden Flowers/Garden Shrubs/House Plants/Plants for Small Gardens/Roses

General Information
Aircraft/Arms and Armour/Coins and Medals/Flags/ Fortune Telling/Freshwater Fishing/Guns/Military Uniforms/Motor Boats and Boating/National Costumes of the world/ Orders and Decorations/Rockets and Missiles/ Sailing/Sailing Ships and Sailing Craft/Sea Fishing/Trains/Veteran and Vintage Cars/Warships

History and Mythology
Age of Shakespeare/Archaeology/Discovery of: Africa/ The American West/Australia/Japan/North America/South America/Great Land Battles/Great Naval Battles/Myths and Legends of: Africa/Ancient Egypt/Ancient Greece/Ancient Rome/India/The South Seas/Witchcraft and Black Magic

Natural History
The Animal Kingdom/Animals of Australia and New Zealand/Animals of Southern Asia/Bird Behaviour/Birds of Prey/Butterflies/Evolution of Life/Fishes of the world/ Fossil Man/A Guide to the Seashore/Life in the Sea/Mammals of the world/Monkeys and Apes/Natural History Collecting/The Plant Kingdom/Prehistoric Animals/Seabirds/Seashells/Snakes of the world/Trees of the world/Tropical Birds/Wild Cats

Popular Science
Astronomy/Atomic Energy/Chemistry/Computers at Work/ The Earth/Electricity/Electronics/Exploring the Planets/Heredity The Human Body/Mathematics/Microscopes and Microscopic Life/Physics/Undersea Exploration/The Weather Guide